the joy of
LIVING WITH PLANTS

the joy of
LIVING WITH PLANTS

IDEAS AND INSPIRATIONS FOR INDOOR GARDENS

isabelle palmer

CICO BOOKS
LONDON NEW YORK

To my Grandmother,
my guiding light

This edition published in 2021 by CICO Books
an imprint of Ryland Peters & Small
20–21 Jockey's Fields, London WC1R 4BW
341 E 116th St, New York, NY, 10029

First published in 2016 as *House Plants*

www.rylandpeters.com

10 9 8 7 6 5 4 3 2 1

A CIP catalog record for this book is
available from the Library of Congress
and the British Library.

ISBN: 978 1 80065 027 5

Printed in China

Copy editor: Caroline West
Designer: Mark Latter
Photographer: Helen Cathcart
Stylist: Marisa Daly

Art director: Sally Powell
Production manager: Gordana Simakovic
Publishing manager: Penny Craig
Publisher: Cindy Richards

CONTENTS

introduction

Living in the city, I am very aware that outdoor space is at a premium. During the winter, while looking out at my balconies and dreaming of the summer, I started thinking: what if you wanted to have that little bit of green, but didn't have any outside space at all? This turned my attention indoors. The "house plant," once an integral part of homes everywhere, had gone out of fashion. However, I've noticed a renewed interest in house gardening. Even if you live in the country, indoor plants can offer some much-needed contact with nature, something that is very important, not only in terms of aesthetics, but also to promote a healthy emotional environment. House plants bring their natural form, color, and fragrance to the home, and can add the finishing touch to many interior schemes.

Historically, plants have been used indoors for centuries—indeed, medieval paintings depict Crusaders returning with plant specimens from many corners of the world. The Victorian period in the nineteenth century was a golden age of plant collecting, which went hand in hand with the Victorians' passion for exploration and discovery. The Victorian plant hunters were seen as adventurers traveling to remote areas to bring back exotic plants from around the world. This era also saw a rise in popularity of terrariums and Wardian cases. The legacy of these Victorian plant explorers lives on in the plants that thrive in our modern natural landscape.

In this book, I will show you how to choose, grow, and decorate with house plants, as well as guide you through the different techniques needed to care for your new "green guests."

there is nothing more pleasing than bringing greenery into your home. Not only are plants beautiful but many can clean household air and balance humidity

tools & techniques

This may be your first foray into nurturing house plants, or you may be a seasoned pro. Even so, most people need to look afresh at their house plant displays now and then, so, although you may be using this book only as a source of inspirational ideas, I will cover the basics of growing house plants from start to finish, as this is a book for both the beginner and the experienced gardener. The main requirements for growing healthy house plants are a well-lit, draft-free spot with an even temperature and reasonably high humidity. However, some plants have specific needs, and this section will show you how to care for them.

TOOLS AND MATERIALS

The tools and materials you use are really important when caring for and maintaining your house plants. You don't need to spend a fortune, however, as many tools can be made from household spoons, forks, and knives with a bit of tape and a long stick. Here, I have outlined the most useful tools for all the projects in this book.

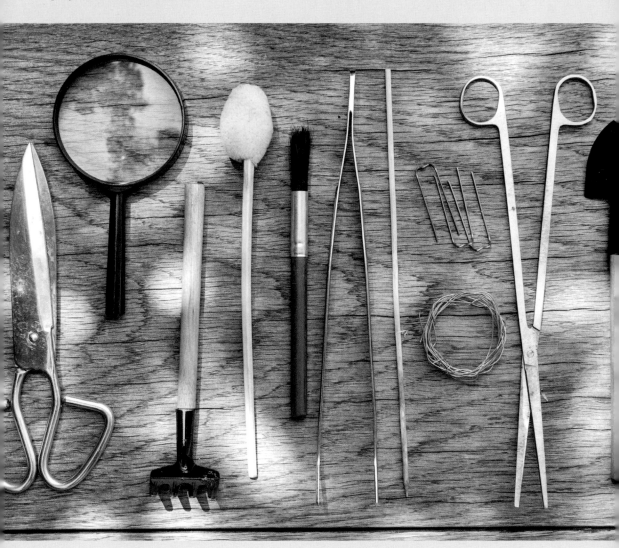

useful tools

❖ *Mini spades or trowels* for digging holes and moving objects in containers.

❖ *Mini rake* for raking over and patting down the potting mix.

❖ *Sticks* are great for moving and positioning plants in difficult areas and also for making holes in the potting mix when you are sowing seeds.

❖ *Stiff paper* for making a funnel to pour materials into small, difficult-to-access containers.

❖ *Long-handled tweezers* are useful for grabbing plants when you're positioning them in small containers.

❖ *A magnifying glass* is helpful for enlarging small objects when planting up a terrarium.

❖ *Scissors* are one of the most useful tools, as you will find them really helpful for deadheading, trimming back, tidying up, pruning, and taking cuttings.

❖ *Long-handled scissors* are great for pruning and tweaking off dead leaves.

❖ *Leaf pruners* are really useful for cutting more woody and mature plant stems that cannot be cut with a pair of scissors.

❖ *Root clippers* are a great tool when you're repotting plants (especially bonsai) and also for propagating plants by division.

❖ *Homemade glass cleaner* for cleaning difficult-to-reach areas inside pots, glass vases, and terrariums. To make your own, simply stick a small sponge onto the end of a chopstick.

❖ *Small brushes* are useful for brushing stray potting mix from leaves.

❖ *Bamboo sticks and trellis* are ideal for providing plants such as climbers with a form of support, and for training plants.

❖ *Wire* for training plants, such as *Passiflora* (passionflower) and *Hedera* (ivy), as well as for tying in untidy branches. A good green-coated floristry wire is perfect, as the green will blend in with the plant.

❖ *Floristry pins* are great for holding down mosses and fixing parts of clump moss together.

❖ *A ball of string* is useful for securing climbing plants and fixing moss around plants, such as in the hanging fruit garden project (see page 112).

❖ *Plant labels* are helpful when sowing different seeds, so that you can remember what they are.

❖ *Spray bottles* can be used for misting plants, as well as for treating pests with pesticides or fungicides.

TOP 10 HOUSE GARDENING TIPS

Here are a few useful guidelines to help you start growing plants in your home:

1 Position plants carefully
Choose plants that suit the environment, since even the most dedicated gardener can't make a sun-loving plant thrive in a cold, shady area. So, ensure that your plants are suited to the light levels and temperature of the room in which they'll be positioned.

2 Try to avoid direct sun
Windowsills in direct sunlight will be too hot for most house plants. Also, don't place house plants over direct sources of heat, such as radiators.

3 Avoid shady areas
Ensure there is sufficient light for your house plants to photosynthesize effectively.

4 Avoid temperature extremes
Keep delicate plants away from drafts, since these will decrease humidity levels.

5 Pot on regularly
Aim to repot your house plants into larger pots every two years or so. This will ensure that they are not stressed and will thrive.

6 Be well equipped

Use the proper tools for indoor gardening. A long-spouted watering can and a mister to increase humidity are both essential for reducing dust levels, as well as dealing with pest and disease outbreaks. A long-handled fork and a pair of scissors are great for accessing difficult areas, while a sponge attached to a long handle will keep glass containers clean.

7 Water wisely

Don't overwater house plants; adding some drainage material at the bottom of the pot will help to keep roots aerated and ensure that they don't drown.

8 Winter dormancy

Allow house plants to rest during the winter period and move them to a cooler position. This is because most plants are dormant at this time, and so don't need as much sunlight. You should also reduce the amount of water and food you provide, as this can help to prevent diseases such as mold and root rot. Move plants away from windows, because these areas will be too cold in the winter.

9 Be vigilant

Learn to recognize potential problems early on, before a pest infestation or other physiological problem kills off your plant. For example, danger signs for low air humidity include flower buds falling off, leaves withering, and leaves with brown tips. Signs of high humidity include mold, rot, and soft growth.

10 Think long-term

Some popular house plant gifts only have a short growing period, so choose plants that will thrive for longer if you want a year-round display.

GETTING STARTED

Knowing a little about the processes by which plants live can be useful. Living indoors is not natural for plants, so it's essential that you don't inhibit their growth by providing them with the wrong growing conditions.

LIGHT LEVELS

Most house plants, including orchids and bromeliads, thrive in filtered sunlight, but all green-leaved plants such as philodendrons can live happily away from windows and even in the shade. However, variegated- and colored-leaved plants, flowering plants, and cacti and succulents must have good light levels to flower or do well.

light and photosynthesis

The process of photosynthesis provides plants with energy and occurs naturally as a result of the green pigment chlorophyll in their leaves and stems. (Plants such as cacti only have chlorophyll in their stems.) Sunlight acts on the chlorophyll to produce carbohydrates, using carbon dioxide from the air and water from the soil. The carbon dioxide is taken in by stomata (or pores) that are usually found on the underside of the leaves. The light energy splits the water molecules into oxygen and hydrogen. The hydrogen combines with the carbon to produce carbohydrates like glucose that provide the plant with food. Oxygen and water vapor are released into the air as by-products of the process, which is why plants are so beneficial to us indoors.

TEMPERATURE

Every plant has a preferred temperature range in which it will grow well, and it will die if exposed to temperatures outside this range for a long period of time. Central heating or a dry atmosphere can have detrimental effects, drying out and scorching your plants, so avoid placing them in direct sunlight or too near a radiator.

You should also avoid extreme fluctuations in temperature, as this will shock the plant, with adverse effects. Drafts—such as those found on window ledges and near outside doors—will cause increased transpiration and rapidly dry out your plants. As a guide, bear the following ideal temperatures in mind when growing house plants:

❖ The minimum winter temperature (and for winter dormancy) is 55°F (12°C).

❖ The average temperature for plants to thrive is 65–75°F (18–24°C).

❖ Plants from less tropical regions grow well in 50–60°F (10–16°C).

❖ Fluctuations of 20°F (11°C) or more within 24 hours are detrimental to all plants, so keep temperatures constant.

❖ Young seedlings will grow best in a constant temperature.

HUMIDITY

It is advisable to match the humidity levels to the plant; for example, cacti need a dry atmosphere. If you wish to raise the humidity, try grouping plants together in one place. Regular misting will also help to increase humidity and aid plant growth.

CHOOSING AND POSITIONING CONTAINERS

When choosing a container for your house plant, the most important consideration is to ensure that your plant and pot are in proportion. Your choice will inevitably be influenced by personal preference, but you should also take the time to check that the container will work aesthetically where you are going to position it.

TYPES OF CONTAINER

Your new house plant will probably come in a plastic pot, unless you are buying one that has already been planted up in its "smart" container. This is when you can choose a container that reflects your personal style and surroundings. It is very important to check that the container has holes at the bottom so that water can drain away and so prevent the plant from rotting. Also, if you are grouping plants together, make sure that the containers match and preferably group them in odd numbers to enhance the aesthetics of the arrangement. I tend to use simple pots, that is, nothing too fussy and highly patterned, as I feel this detracts from the impact of the plant.

TERRARIUMS

Terrariums are great for growing indoor plants in today's centrally heated and air-conditioned homes. Growing plants in a closed glass case, or terrarium, means that water evaporating from the leaves during transpiration condenses on the glass and then trickles down the sides of the case to be reabsorbed by the roots.

Unlike their Victorian predecessors, terrariums today are both affordable and suitable for smaller houses and apartments. They are a wonderful way to keep succulents and cacti indoors, preventing them from rotting or drying out. Easy to set up, they make a great project for the whole family.

You'll need to decide whether you would like your terrarium to be open or closed. Open terrariums can tolerate some direct sunlight, but be aware that too much sun may burn any leaves that are in direct contact with the sides of the terrarium. In contrast, closed terrariums need a location where they will receive bright light, but no direct sunlight. If they are placed in direct sunlight, the temperature inside the terrarium can rise considerably and "cook" the plants. (A closed terrarium may also be an open terrarium that has a cover.)

Whether you opt for an open or closed terrarium should also be determined by your choice of plants—sun-loving plants yearn for natural light, so use an open terrarium, while plants that require high levels of humidity need a closed terrarium. Mind-your-own-business (*Soleirolia soleirolii*), violas, mosses, and cacti and succulents will all grow well in any type of terrarium.

GLASS VASES

It is unusual to grow plants in potting mix in a glass container, as their roots don't fare well when exposed to the light. However, they make great receptacles for creating water gardens and growing aquatic plants. Adding some pebbles helps to reduce the light levels, and so these are widely used in glass containers.

CLAY CONTAINERS

Containers made from clay or terracotta can prove both practical and versatile when you're growing house plants. You can choose terracotta pots in their natural color or paint them to blend in with your décor or environment. Because terracotta is a porous material, the pots lose water from their sides, as well as from the base, so may need watering more frequently. Using a decorative mulch or topping can help to reduce excess evaporation.

WOODEN CRATES

A wooden crate makes a great partner for lush foliage plants and can be kept natural or painted to match your environment. Wood is not watertight, however, so you will also need to give the crate a plastic lining. Be careful when watering, because you don't want the plants' roots to become waterlogged. Alternatively, you can make a few holes in the base of the crate to allow excess water to escape, but take care that draining water doesn't cause any damage to the surface the crate sits on.

HANGING OBJECTS

Even if space is at a premium, you can still introduce interesting foliage into your home by using hanging objects as containers. They can also make a striking focal point in a room.

WINDOW BOXES

A window box is a great way to use space on your window ledges, both inside and out. Choose boxes that complement your space.

HANDMADE OBJECTS

You will derive a great deal of pride and pleasure from making your own containers, whether you are just reusing household items or making them from scratch. I have used a variety of handmade objects in the book, so look through the projects to see if you feel there are any you would enjoy making yourself.

CHINA AND PORCELAIN CONTAINERS

These are available in a vast array of shapes and sizes, as well as lots of different colors and designs. When designing a container grouping, I usually make sure that the containers complement one another in all these areas. Using lots of different patterns, colors, and textures not only makes a display look messy and old-fashioned, but can also distract your attention from the plants. China and porcelain containers are unlikely to have drainage holes, so make sure you remove any excess water after watering.

METAL CONTAINERS AND WIRE CRATES

Containers made from metal are wonderfully contemporary and also a great way to recycle unusual objects. Few have drainage holes, but you can easily make these yourself using a drill and drill bit or a hammer and strong nail.

house gardener's tip:

Ceramic pots and saucers can sometimes damage surfaces, so stick on felt, latex (rubber), or foam pad squares to protect your furniture.

GROUPING CONTAINERS

If you decide to group containers together, make sure the pots match or are of the same design or style. Also, consider your choice of plants carefully and think about whether they will look attractive with the pot. A good way to check this before potting up is to place the plant behind the pot and then stand back to see the effect.

When you choose containers for grouping, another useful design concept is to make sure that you have an odd number of planters, so aim for container groups of 3, 5, or 7.

Try to think outside the box and be creative. Indeed, in the section on "Old Finds" (see pages 68–99), I have used lots of recycled objects that are not technically for plants, but are a great way to create an interesting focal point.

There are two main principles for arranging containers: you can either have a symmetrical arrangement with one large container and two smaller ones on either side, or you can make the arrangement asymmetrical by positioning both smaller containers on one side of a larger one.

POTTING MIXES

Most indoor plants will thrive in sterile, soil-less potting mix (either peat- or peat-substitute-based). It is not recommended that you use garden soil, as it may contain weed seeds or diseases. Potting mix is sterile and does not contain any fungi, weeds, pests, soil-borne diseases, seeds, or toxins to prevent your plants from growing well.

Specialty potting mixes are also available for particular plants with specific needs, including ericaceous potting mix for lime-hating plants, such as camellias, and gritty, fast-draining potting mix for cacti. Coarse, low-nutrient potting mixes, which contain vermiculite and perlite, are ideal for orchids because they need good drainage. This is because orchids are particularly sensitive and don't like getting their roots wet. You can use a seedling potting mix for sowing seeds and growing seedlings.

DECORATIVE TOPPINGS

Using a decorative topping not only finishes off your container aesthetically, but also helps the plant to retain moisture. You will need to move the decorative topping aside slightly when checking if your plant needs watering. I have listed my favorites below, but again, it's a case of personal choice—just remember to match the topping to your container and its surroundings.

* *Moss* is ideal for top-dressing container plantings and there are many different varieties to choose from. Reindeer moss is wonderful used in combination with sand toppings. Sphagnum moss is perfect for covering the potting mix in terrariums. Fern or sheet moss makes a great cover for large-scale planters owing to its size. Water moss balls, which are produced by the churning of rivers, are spherical balls of moss that look striking in water terrariums. Pillow moss—often known as clump or cushion moss—forms neat clumps, which range from small, round mounds to larger, irregularly shaped mounds. Pillow moss is great for making miniature gardens because it looks like rolling fields.

* *Sand* looks lovely on simple story gardens and is particularly nice to use when you're planting up a container as a project with children. I like to use aquatic sands because they give a finer finish and are available in a multitude of colors.

* *Pebbles* are available in various shapes, sizes, and finishes from garden and aquatic centers.

* *Woodchips* are perfect for arrangements that have a more natural, earthy feel.

* *Fine gravel* is great for giving a more organic feel to your planting display.

* *Shells* can be great fun to find on the beach. I pick up many different shells on my trips to the seaside.

* *Slate chips* work well with sleek, modern arrangements.

BASIC TECHNIQUES

When choosing an indoor plant, it's worth doing some research to find out what position it will thrive in best, the growing conditions it needs, and whether it will fit in with the intended environment. This will ensure that your plant remains healthy and that you avoid making costly mistakes.

SELECTING A HEALTHY PLANT

When buying a house plant from a garden center or nursery, take the time to check that you have chosen a healthy specimen that will thrive once you get home. The following checklist should help you to make a good choice:

✳ Look for strong, healthy leaves with a good, vibrant color. Avoid any plant with damaged or blotchy leaves.

✳ The plant's stems should be firm and, if the plant is flowering, choose one that has lots of unopened buds for a longer flowering period.

✳ Check that there is no space between the potting mix and the inside of the pot, because this means the plant is extremely dry and will grow poorly.

✳ Make sure there are no insects or larvae on the plant; you don't want to introduce pest infestations into your home, as these may affect other house plants.

✳ Avoid diseased plants with a furry mold at the base or any unsightly blotches.

✳ Check for any curled or withered leaves, which indicate that the plant won't grow well in future.

✳ Check that there are no soggy, wilted patches, since this suggests that the plant has root rot or is pot-bound.

✳ Check that the roots are not growing out of the bottom of the pot. This means that the plant is pot-bound and so has been under stress.

✳ Buy a younger plant if possible because, although it will be smaller, it will adapt to its new environment better.

✳ When taking your plant home, make sure it is wrapped properly, to ensure that there is no damage to the leaves during transit.

✳ Don't place the plant in direct sunlight for the first few weeks, so that it can acclimatize before you move it to its final position. However, if you are buying a flowering plant, such as a cyclamen, azalea, or chrysanthemum, place it in its final sunny position immediately.

PLANTING A CONTAINER

There will be times when you need to pot up a plant, especially if you purchase it in an ugly plastic container. You may also need to repot a plant in order to give it a new lease of life or when it has outgrown its container.

1 Cover the bottom of the container with a layer of drainage material, such as gravel or pebbles, aiming to fill about a quarter of the container's volume. This will allow the roots to breathe and prevent them from drowning.

2 Fill the container with potting mix to bring the plant up so that the top of the root-ball is just beneath the rim of the container. Try to position the plant centrally in the container and make sure it is not lopsided.

3 Carefully feed more potting mix in between the plant and container, and firm it down. Avoid compacting the potting mix too much, though, as this will hinder drainage.

4 Add a layer of decorative mulch, such as fine gravel or shells, to finish off the planting. Not only does this make the container look more attractive, but it can also help to reduce the rate of evaporation.

TRAINING A STANDARD

This is a great way to transform a plant by pruning it to create a plant with a single stem. A standard is quite a formal way of growing a shrub, which aims to bring the bulk of the ornamental growth up to eye-level. Plants that respond well to this treatment include *Syringa* (lilac), *Laurus nobilis* (bay laurel), and *Lavandula* (lavender).

1 Choose a plant with a strong central stem running from the bottom to the top. I have used a *Citrus japonica* (kumquat) here.

2 Remove the bottom leaves to reveal the stem at the base and cut out any side shoots from the lower part of the plant.

3 If the stem is too thin, you can use a pole or bamboo stick to provide support. Keep the stem free of any new shoots and pinch out any leading leaves in order to keep a balanced, bushy head as the standard develops.

a standard is quite a formal way of growing a shrub, which aims to bring the bulk of the ornamental growth up to eye-level

PLANT CARE

Although plants can withstand fluctuations in their growing conditions for a while, consistent care is essential for the health of your plants.

Succulents, with their reserves, for example, can tolerate a little neglect more readily than a seedling, which has nothing to draw on.

HOW TO WATER

You should water plants more in spring and summer when they are actively growing and less when they are resting in winter. You can check whether a plant needs to be watered by pushing your fingers into the surface of the potting mix to a depth of about ½in (1cm). If the mix is not moist, then the plant needs to be watered. If there is a decorative topping in the container, scrape a little away to reach the potting mix.

There are two ways to water. You can water from above, which is the most convenient method and ensures an even distribution of water. Make sure there is a lip of about 1–1½in (2–3cm) between the potting mix and the top of the pot. This will allow the maximum amount of water to reach the plant. Alternatively, you can water from below, which involves watering the saucer to avoid wetting the crown of the plant and causing it to rot. This is particularly useful for fleshy plants such as cyclamen.

water plants more in spring and summer when they are actively growing and less when they are resting in winter

VACATION WATERING

One of the most common ways to kill a plant is by underwatering it, which can be a problem when you are away. Fortunately, you can use the following techniques to protect them:

* *Capillary matting:* This is readily available from garden centers (I usually find that 3ft/1m is sufficient). Fill the sink about three-quarters full with water and dunk the capillary matting so that it is evenly moist. Then, put one end of the matting in the water and drape the other end over the draining board. This will only work if the potting mix is in contact with the matting, and it won't work on plants with drainage material in the bottom of their containers. Place the pots on the matting.

* *Wick system:* This uses a long, narrow piece of capillary matting. Position a bowl so that it is higher than the level of the potting mix. Fill the bowl with water and put the piece of matting in the water, weighing it down with a stone. Push the other end of the matting into the potting mix.

* *Slow-seepage system:* Take a cut-off water bottle with the lid end intact. Bore a few holes in the lid to allow the water to drain through slowly. Push the lid end into the potting mix, and fill the bottle with water.

INCREASING HUMIDITY

There are a number of ways to increase the level of humidity around plants, such as misting the leaves with water. You can also stand a plant in a tray or saucer and spread a layer of pebbles around it. Fill the saucer with water so that the moist pebbles increase the humidity. Air plants need regular misting since they take their moisture in from the air.

REVIVING A WILTED PLANT

Underwatering can have a dramatic effect on a plant, which seems to wilt overnight. Since the potting mix will probably be coming away from the sides of the container, it's difficult for the plant to absorb any water. To revive it, move it to a cool area, out of direct sunlight, and submerge the container in a bowl of tepid water. Leave to soak for about half an hour and then let the container drain for 10 minutes. (You can weigh the container down with a large pebble if it starts to float up.) The plant should show signs of recovery in about an hour. Soaking the plant in this way will lead to a good rate of transpiration and kick-start the plant into reviving itself.

OVERWATERING

If a plant's leaves turn yellow or begin to fall off, it is likely that you have overwatered it. Remove the plant from the pot and place a couple of layers of newspaper or kitchen paper around the potting mix to absorb excess moisture from the mix. Keep the plant just moist and out of direct sun until the roots recover.

DIPPING AND DRAINING

Some plants, such as orchids, are planted in a loose potting mix, making it hard to tell when they need watering. You can remedy this by using the dip-and-drain technique once a week. Simply dip the plant (in its pot) into a bowl or pitcher of tepid water for about 10 minutes, then leave on a draining board for about 20 minutes to allow excess water to drain from the potting mix.

FEEDING

Feeding indoor plants is essential if they are to remain healthy. There are three major constituents of plant food: nitrogen (N) for leaf growth and "greening" up yellowing plants; phosphorous (P) for root growth; and potassium (K) for flowers. Other important ingredients in plant fertilizers are the trace elements, which are generally present in most (but not all) compound fertilizers. When buying a plant fertilizer, remember to look at the ingredients, as these must be listed by law.

Feeding is generally carried out only during the growing season, when watering frequency is high. If you have just repotted your plant, you have a couple of months before the food in the potting mix runs out. Most plants benefit from a feed once every two to four weeks. The tip is not to miss a few applications and then give lots of food in compensation, since this will cause more problems, such as wilting leaves. There are three main ways of feeding your house plants:

ABOVE Clockwise from top left: Powder feed, fertilizer granules, liquid feed.

* ***Powder and liquid feeds:*** These are diluted with water and applied at regular intervals when you water the plants. A balanced liquid feed will meet the needs of most plants, but there are also specialty formulas available for plants such as orchids, citrus plants, and ericaceous (lime-hating) plants.

* ***Fertilizer granules:*** These are added to the potting mix when you plant up the container. Also available are clusters of granules that you can push into the potting mix.

* ***Fertilizer sticks:*** These are simply pushed into the potting mix to provide a slowly released supply of nutrients.

APPLYING A TOP-DRESSING

You can refresh your house plants by applying a new top-dressing. Simply remove a couple of inches of the old potting mix from the top of the container. Insert some slow-release fertilizer and refill with new potting mix. Water in well.

BOOSTING LIGHT LEVELS

The amount of light your plants get can be increased by keeping their leaves clean, allowing the maximum amount of light to be absorbed. Use a damp cloth or sponge-stick to wipe away dirt and other residue. Use a soft brush to clean away dust gently; this is particularly useful for cacti, as you can get in between the spines.

POTTING ON

The term "potting on" refers to the transfer of seedlings and cuttings to their first pot and a permanent position, but it also means potting a plant into a larger pot where it will have ample room to grow. While the root systems of plants growing in the open garden have a free run and are not constrained, container plants eventually outgrow their pots, and these cramped conditions can result in a pot-bound plant. This is where the root system has become ingrown, wrapping itself around the pot and creating an impenetrable wall. As a result, the plants cannot access sufficient water or nutrients.

1 Water the plant well an hour before potting on so that it will be easier to remove from its pot. Carefully remove the plant from the pot and gently tease out the roots so that they can grow into the surrounding potting mix.

2 Fill the new pot with a layer of drainage material and then a base layer of new potting mix.

3 Place the plant in its new pot and fill in the sides with more potting mix. Add a layer of potting mix on top, too. Firm down so that there is about 1in (2.5cm) between the top of the potting mix and the rim of the pot. Give the plant a good water.

PRUNING

The main reasons for pruning are what are often referred to as "the three Ds": removing dead, damaged, or diseased stems. Plants with a bushy formation will need their growing points and side branches pruned to maintain their structure. You can also keep structural plants neat by regular pruning, and encourage further blooms on flowering plants by deadheading. Pruning can be done at any time it is needed, but the best time is in spring, when new growth is more vigorous. Here are a few helpful pruning techniques to get you started:

* *Making pruning cuts:* You can either make a slanted cut just above an outward-facing bud or make a straight cut across the stem above a pair of opposite buds. This is critical because you don't want to make the cut too near the bud and damage it, while making a cut too far away from the bud may promote disease in the stem.

* *Pinching out:* Natural growth hormones are found in the highest concentrations in the growing tips of the plant, where they act to suppress growth from the lower parts of the plant. If you remove the growing tips, the hormones in the other parts of the plant are triggered into producing side shoots at almost every leaf axil (the angle between the upper surface of a branch or leafstalk and the stem from which it grows.) So, pinching out in this way encourages a plant to produce dense, bushy growth. Use your finger and thumb to pinch out growing tips on climbing plants. Hand pruners (secateurs) can be used on plants that have tougher stems.

* *Deadheading:* Plants usually stop growing once they have set seed, so removing spent flowers encourages new buds to develop because of a plant's natural instinct to produce seed. Removing tired flowers will also reduce the risk of petals falling onto leaves and causing rot. Cut off as much of the flower as possible.

PROPAGATION

You can propagate indoor plants in a number of different ways, including sowing seed, taking cuttings, dividing plants, removing offsets, and grafting.

try *growing*
campanula,
wisteria, or coleus
from seed

SOWING SEED

Starting plants from seed is a very economical way to obtain more house plants.

Suitable plants: Campanula, wisteria (for bonsai), and coleus.

1 Prepare a pot with a layer of drainage material such as pebbles or stone chippings over the base, filling about a quarter of the pot's volume, then fill with potting mix to just below the rim of the pot.

2 Distribute the seeds evenly over the surface of the potting mix, cover with a piece of glass, and place a saucer filled with water beneath the pot. This will provide a good environment for the seeds to germinate. Place in a sunny position, and wait for the seeds to germinate.

3 Once the seeds have germinated, prop up the piece of glass with a support to allow air to circulate.

4 When the seedlings have 2 pairs of leaves, gently tip out the pot to allow easy access to the seedlings. Replant the seedlings in seed trays, using a dibble (dibber) or pencil to make small planting holes in the new potting mix. This will ensure that the seedlings are equally spaced. Follow the instructions on the seed packet for the sowing distance for the type of plant. Gently firm more potting mix around the base of the seedlings, and leave them to mature.

5 Once the seedlings are established, you can pot them up into their own individual pots.

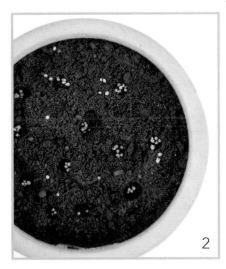

2

3

STEM AND LEAF CUTTINGS

Taking a cutting involves removing a piece of the parent plant, such as a leaf, stem or root, in order to grow a new plant. Taking cuttings is called vegetative propagation, and is the easiest method of propagating plants.

* ***Stem cuttings:*** Some plants, such as crassulas, azaleas, and camellias, are easier to propagate from stem cuttings than others, and the cutting needs only to be placed in water to produce roots. Others will need a little help from a hormone rooting powder to re-root. Propagation by stem cuttings is the most commonly used method to propagate many woody ornamental plants. Stem cuttings from many popular shrubs are quite easy to root, although stem cuttings from tree species are usually more difficult to root.

In general, you should take cuttings from the current or past season's growth. Avoid material with flower buds if possible. Remove any flowers and flower buds when you are preparing a cutting so that the cutting's energy can be used to produce new roots rather than flowers. Take cuttings from healthy, disease-free plants, preferably from the upper part of the plant.

Suitable plants: *Crassula, Camellia, Epipremnum aureum* (devil's ivy), and *Hedera* (ivy).

ABOVE: Stem and leaf cuttings

BELOW: A succulent offset

* ***Leaf cuttings:*** Some plants can be increased by using their leaves. Part-leaf cutting involves cutting a leaf along its length by the central vein and then placing the leaf lengthwise in potting mix. New shoots should pop up along the cut. Once the cuttings are established, they can be transplanted to new pots. A whole-leaf cutting is where a whole leaf with a stem attached—perhaps from a succulent—is removed and the end pushed into some moist potting mix. New shoots should appear from the stem of the parent plant—these are called offsets.

Suitable plants: *Streptocarpus, Sedum, Sansevieria, Eucomis, Crassula,* and *Begonia masoniana.*

OFFSETS

Offsets should not be separated from the parent plant until they are well established. When the offsets resemble the parent plant in form and shape, separate them by using a knife to cut as close to the parent plant as possible. The offsets can then be repotted in moist potting mix.

Suitable plants: Cacti and succulents.

DIVISION

Sansevierias, ferns, cacti, and orchids all have a clump of roots that can easily be divided to produce more plants. The new plants can then be planted up in individual pots. Simply select a point where you want to divide the plant and use a knife to separate the root-ball carefully. Make sure that you don't cause any damage, as this will affect the plant's roots and it may die.

Suitable plants: Sansevieria, *Hedera* (ivy), *Soleirolia soleirolii* (mind-your-own-business).

sansevierias, ferns, cacti, and orchids have roots that can easily be **divided** to produce **more** plants

GRAFTING

Grafting, or hybridization, is a particularly useful method of propagation for cacti. It involves taking one part of a cactus and grafting it onto another cactus to create a more interesting formation. To graft a cactus, use a knife to cut a V-shaped groove in the base plant. Replicate this in the graft with a pointed V so that it will fit inside the groove. Take a toothpick or a piece of wire and drive it vertically through the two plants to secure them together.

Suitable plants: Cacti and succulents.

CHOOSING AND PLACING PLANTS

The grouping, arranging, and placing of plants is an art form and should be approached in the same way as you design your home—it's really a question of personal style and taste, and not subject to strict rules. However, it is important to follow a few golden rules when you're planting and positioning containers. As well as matching the plant to its container in terms of scale and design, and taking the surrounding décor into consideration, you'll also have to choose the right plant for the right place in terms of light levels, temperature, and humidity. For example, are you planning to site your house plant in a sunny or a shady spot? Do you need a plant for the bathroom or kitchen, or perhaps a drafty hallway? Although the list is not intended to be exhaustive, here I have recommended a few reliable plants for the different conditions and rooms in the home.

KEY PLANTS FOR SUNNY POSITIONS

Placing a plant on a windowsill where it will receive direct sunlight may cause the sap to overheat and damage the plant's cells. The plants listed below are some that will grow well in bright, sunny positions. Direct sun indoors for a long period of time is detrimental to plants because the glass magnifies the sun's rays.

Ficus binnendijkii
"Amstel King"
This fig is ideal for a bright position. Large leaves with a red tint on the new growth adorn this lush, robust variety. It makes a pleasing alternative to *Ficus benjamina* (weeping fig).
SITE: Bright, indirect light to bright shade. Will tolerate a small amount of direct sun.
TEMPERATURE: Average room temperature (65–75°F/18–24°C).
WATERING: Water regularly in the growing season, but leave to dry out slightly first. Water only rarely over winter. Benefits from an occasional misting.
FEEDING: Apply a liquid feed every month or so.
TIP: *Prune to shape in winter if required.*

Hibiscus rosa-sinensis
Rose mallow
This beautiful tropical shrub will enhance any room or indoor garden. Many colorful, flowering, tropical bush plants can be used in an indoor tropical garden. They provide a perfect flower base for indoor gardening.
SITE: Prefers direct sun, but not fierce sunlight.
TEMPERATURE: Average room temperature (65–75°F/18–24°C).
WATERING: Water regularly in the growing season, but leave to dry out slightly first.
FEEDING: Apply a liquid feed once a month.
TIP: *Hard pruning leads to the production of many side shoots that flower prolifically.*

Sansevieria trifasciata var. *laurentii*
Variegated snake plant
Sansevierias are perfect plants for the modern interior. Boasting long, sword-like leaves with an elegant gold trim, they can reach 3ft (1m) in height and provide strong structure if placed in a group.
SITE: Will tolerate a range of conditions, from full sun to light shade.
TEMPERATURE: Average room temperature (65–75°F/18–24°C).
WATERING: Water when the potting mix is dry, and less over winter. No need for high humidity.
FEEDING: Apply a liquid feed every month or two.
TIP: *A good suggestion is to pot on when the roots have completely filled the pot. It can then be divided and replanted.*

Yucca elephantipes
Spineless yucca
Yuccas tolerate full sun.
SITE: Thrives in a bright position and will tolerate direct sun. Although yuccas tolerate some shade, spin the plant around from time to time or the branches will lean toward the light.
TEMPERATURE: Being fairly hardy, it will thrive in most situations.
WATERING: Keep well watered in summer, but water infrequently in winter. The more you water over the summer, the faster the plant will grow. It's advisable to let the plant dry out before watering again.
FEEDING: Apply a liquid feed every three weeks or so over summer (less if you want to restrict growth).
TIP: *Use a free-draining potting mix. The plant can be put outside over the summer months.*

Zamioculcas zamiifolia
ZZ plant
Each of the branches growing from the potting mix is, in fact, a leaf and the "leaves" are leaflets growing out of them. An easy plant for almost every room.
SITE: Prefers light shade, although it will tolerate some sun as well.
TEMPERATURE: Average room temperature, but not below 65°F (18°C) in winter.
WATERING: Allow the surface of the potting mix to dry out before re-watering. Water sparingly over winter.
FEEDING: Apply a very weak liquid feed every month or so over the growing season.
TIPS: *The ZZ plant can be divided and replanted when repotting is required. Do not let the plant get too wet, as rotting can occur over the winter if it is over-watered.*

KEY PLANTS FOR SHADY POSITIONS

Plants will not grow where they receive too little light because they cannot photosynthesize properly. The leaves of variegated plants have less chlorophyll in the lighter sections, which means that they require more light than plants with darker leaves that can tolerate a shadier spot. Flowering plants in particular need sufficient light to flower well. Plants also grow best in environments that are stable, so don't position them near doors because they may suffer from drafts and their leaves may be damaged as you move past. Shady, drafty conditions typically occur in hallways, so choose plants with care for this part of your home.

Aloe vera

Thriving without the need for much care, this plant is an ideal choice for busy or absent-minded plant-lovers.
SITE: Aloes will thrive in sun, but may turn brown in harsh light. Indirect sunlight is best.
TEMPERATURE: Average room temperature (65–75°F/18–24°C).
WATERING: Avoid overwatering, because this is a succulent. Allow the potting mix to become fairly dry before you water again. Water lightly during the winter months as the potting mix will dry out more slowly.
FEEDING: Feed at about a quarter of the usual dilution once a month over the growing season.
TIP: *The gel found inside this plant is cooling and soothing for all sorts of*

BELOW: *Hedera helix* (ivy)

skin problems, including burns, cuts, stings, bruises, and rashes, as well as for welts, itching, blisters, infections, and abrasions.

Calathea species

Although fairly common as house plants, calatheas are still a stunning genus of plants. With bold leaf markings, as well as the bonus of purple undersides to the leaves, they are a great choice for a shady room.
SITE: Light shade in summer. Brighter conditions are ideal in winter, but keep out of direct sun because this can dull the color of the leaves and damage the plant.
TEMPERATURE: Keep warm (at a minimum temperature of 60°F/16°C).
WATERING: Keep well watered in the summer, making sure that the potting mix is kept moist. Calatheas also enjoy high levels of humidity and so will need regular misting. Brown tips on the leaves indicate that the humidity is too low.
FEEDING: Feed with a very weak solution (half the recommended strength) when watering.
TIP: *Do not repot too often, and use a peat-substitute-based potting mix.*

Campanula species

This pretty flower is easy to grow indoors. It simply requires cool air, moist potting mix, and indirect sunlight. If it is cared for well, you can expect masses of violet-blue flowers from mid- to late summer right through fall (autumn).

SITE: Bright indirect light. Some direct sun in winter is fine.
TEMPERATURE: Cool to average room temperature (45–65°F/7–18°C).
WATERING: Keep the potting mix moist, but not soggy, while the plant is growing and flowering. Soggy potting mix will cause root rot. After flowering, allow the potting mix almost to dry out between waterings.
FEEDING: Feed fortnightly from spring through fall with a balanced liquid fertilizer diluted to half strength.
TIP: *Deadhead to prolong flowering.*

Hedera helix

Ivy

These lush, trailing vines have decorative, lobed leaves.
SITE: Bright light, but not direct sun. If a variegated variety of ivy changes to mostly green, then it isn't receiving enough light.
TEMPERATURE: Tolerates a wide range of temperatures.
WATERING: Keep the potting mix evenly moist, but not soggy, from spring through fall (autumn), and slightly drier in winter.
FEEDING: Feed monthly from spring through fall with a high-nitrogen liquid fertilizer.
TIP: *If you want to keep your ivy plant within bounds, light pruning can be done at any time of the year.*

Narcissus species
Daffodil

Growing daffodils indoors will bring a bright splash of spring-fresh flowers to your home in spring.

SITE: Bright, indirect light. Rotate the pot once in a while because growing daffodils tend to lean toward the light source.

TEMPERATURE: Tolerate cool, draftier conditions (ideal temperature is 60°F/16°C).

WATERING: Keep the potting mix lightly moist. Growing daffodils are thirsty, so it's a good idea to check the potting mix regularly.

FEEDING: Feed fortnightly with a balanced liquid fertilizer diluted to half strength.

TIP: Daffodil bulbs cannot be forced a second time indoors. You can transplant the bulbs outdoors, but it may be two to three years before they bloom again.

Saxifraga stolonifera
Strawberry saxifrage

This plant grows in a mound of rounded, scalloped leaves with decorative silvery veins. The leaves are hairy with burgundy-red undersides.

SITE: Prefers bright light all year round. Some direct morning sun is fine, but protect from strong sun, which can cause the leaves to fade.

TEMPERATURE: Increase levels of humidity in warmer conditions (anything from 50–75°F/10–24°C).

WATERING: Water thoroughly and allow the top inch or so of potting mix to dry out between waterings. Water less frequently in winter when growth is slower.

FEEDING: Feed monthly in spring and summer with a balanced liquid fertilizer diluted to half strength.

TIP: Dry potting mix can cause dry leaves. Aim to keep the potting mix lightly moist.

Spathiphyllum species
Peace lily

This flowering house plant from South America is very easy to care for. It tolerates average indoor conditions better than many house plants.

SITE: Tolerates lightly shaded areas.

TEMPERATURE: Average room temperature (65–75°F/18–24°C).

WATERING: Keep the potting mix evenly moist. Use a pot with a good drainage hole to prevent soggy potting mix, which can cause root rot.

FEEDING: Feed monthly in spring and summer with a balanced liquid fertilizer diluted to half strength.

TIP: This plant is poisonous. Keep it away from children and pets who may play with or chew on parts of the plant. Wash your hands thoroughly after handling it.

Tolmiea menziesii "Taff's Gold"
Piggyback plant

This plant has creamy green foliage all through the year.

SITE: Moderate to bright light, but no direct sun.

TEMPERATURE: Cool to average room temperature (50–75°F/10–24°C).

WATERING: Water regularly throughout the growing season, keeping the potting mix evenly moist, but not soggy.

FEEDING: Feed monthly in spring and summer with a balanced liquid fertilizer diluted to half strength.

TIP: Spikes of tubular flowers sometimes appear in summer, but rarely on plants that are grown indoors.

Tradescantia "Isis"
Spider lily

These plants can be trailing or tufted perennials, usually with fleshy, evergreen foliage and distinctive three-petaled flowers.

SITE: Place in partial shade.

TEMPERATURE: Average to warm room temperature (65–80°F/18–27°C).

WATERING: Water thoroughly, and then allow the top inch or so of potting mix to dry out between waterings.

FEEDING: Feed monthly in spring and summer with a balanced liquid fertilizer diluted to half strength.

TIP: Pot on to a larger pot in spring.

Yucca species

These are very tolerant architectural plants.

SITE: Bright light to full sun.

TEMPERATURE: Cool to average room temperature (50–75°F/10–24°C).

WATERING: Keep the potting mix moist in spring through fall (autumn). In winter, water just enough to prevent the potting mix from drying out.

FEEDING: Feed fortnightly with a balanced liquid fertilizer in spring and summer.

TIP: You can put yuccas outside for summer where they will get some direct sun each day. Outdoors, they may produce tall spikes of fragrant white flowers.

KEY PLANTS FOR THE BATHROOM

The atmosphere in bathrooms tends to vary, being wildly hot and steamy one minute and then cool and dry the next. The humidity can be high because of the steam, so plants must be able to withstand fluctuating temperatures.

Achimenes species

The flowers of these plants appear on short stems that grow from the leaf axils.

SITE: Keep out of direct sunlight.

TEMPERATURE: Average room temperature (65–75°F/18–24°C). Achimenes will tolerate temperatures as low as 55°F (12°C), but anything above 80°F (25°C) will cause the flower buds to shrivel and dry up.

WATERING: Keep the potting mix evenly moist at all times. If the growing medium is allowed to dry out, the plant will become dormant. Do not water in winter.

FEEDING: Feed fortnightly while the plants are blooming with a high-phosphorous liquid fertilizer diluted to a quarter strength.

TIP: *Achimenes will go dormant in winter. When flowering tapers off in the fall (autumn), reduce watering and allow the plant to die back naturally.*

Adiantum species
Maidenhair fern

Maidenhair ferns are foliage plants with arching, black, wiry fronds covered with triangular green leaflets called pinnae.

SITE: Moderate to bright light. No direct sun.

TEMPERATURE: Average room temperature (60–75°F/16–24°C).

WATERING: Do not allow the roots of these ferns to become too wet or to dry out.

FEEDING: Feed once a month from spring through summer with a liquid fertilizer diluted to half strength.

TIP: *This tropical native demands high levels of humidity that are not practical in most homes. For this reason, these plants are best grown in terrariums where humidity is naturally high.*

Aphelandra squarrosa
Zebra plant

This plant is highly recommended for its dramatic foliage and beautiful bright yellow flowers.

SITE: Bright light, but no direct sun. Wrinkled or curled leaves indicate that the plant is getting too much light.

TEMPERATURE: Warm room temperature (65–80°F/18–27°C) all year round.

WATERING: Keep the potting mix evenly moist all year round. Dry potting mix will cause the leaves to wilt or drop off.

FEEDING: Feed monthly in spring and summer with a balanced liquid fertilizer diluted to half strength.

TIP: *Wipe the leaves regularly with a damp cloth to keep them glossy and dust-free.*

Asparagus densiflorus
Sprengeri Group
Asparagus fern

This is not a true fern, but a member of the lily family.

SITE: Bright light, but avoid direct sunlight because it may scorch the foliage.

TEMPERATURE: Average room temperature (60–75°F/16–24°C).

WATERING: Water thoroughly, allowing the potting mix to dry out a little between waterings. Water sparingly in winter, but do not allow the potting mix to dry out completely.

FEEDING: Apply a liquid fertilizer in summer. There is no need for a great amount of care for this plant.

TIP: *Keep your asparagus fern where it'll get filtered light.*

Dracaena sanderiana
Lucky bamboo

A striking plant with a slender, upright stem and graceful, arching green leaves. This indoor plant is very easy to care for. It can be grown in a vase of water with pebbles to keep it upright.

SITE: Bright light, but no direct sun, which will scorch the leaves.

TEMPERATURE: Average room temperature (60–75°F/16–24°C).

WATERING: Change the water every week or two.

FEEDING: Feed every two months with an all-purpose liquid fertilizer. Just a drop will do.

TIP: *This plant is sensitive to chlorine, fluoride, and other chemicals often found in tap water. Use distilled or bottled water only.*

Exacum affine
Persian violet

This is a beautiful flowering house plant.

SITE: Bright light. Some direct morning sun is fine, but keep out of hot afternoon sunlight, which may scorch the plant.

TEMPERATURE: Average room temperature (65–75°F/18–24°C). Keep the plant away from drafts.

WATERING: Keep the potting mix evenly moist, but not soggy.

FEEDING: Feed fortnightly while the plant is blooming with a balanced liquid fertilizer diluted to half strength.

TIP: *Pick off faded flowers to extend the flowering period.*

Nephrolepis exaltata
Boston fern, sword fern
The Boston fern acts as a natural humidifier, absorbing common air pollutants and releasing water vapor.
SITE: Moderate to bright light. No direct sun. Give the plant a quarter turn every week or so to expose all sides to the light.
TEMPERATURE: Average room temperature (60–75°F/16–24°C).
WATERING: Keep the potting mix constantly moist, but not soggy. Watch large ferns and hanging-basket ferns because they can dry out quickly.
FEEDING: Feed fortnightly all year round with a balanced liquid fertilizer diluted to half strength.
TIP: *Fronds that are yellow and wilted are a sign of over-watering. Reduce the amount of water and trim off damaged fronds.*

Peperomia species
This compact plant has short stems covered with heart-shaped, deeply ridged leaves. The leaves are green, sometimes with a blush of red, and have dark green veins.
SITE: Low to bright light. No direct sun.
TEMPERATURE: Average room temperature (65–75°F/18–24°C).
WATERING: Keep only barely moist at all times.
FEEDING: Feed monthly from spring through fall (autumn) with a balanced liquid fertilizer diluted to half strength.
TIP: *Leaf drop may be caused by a build-up of salts in the potting mix from soft water or too much fertilizer.*

Polyscias fruticosa
Ming aralia
Interior designers love the ming aralia because it resembles a Japanese maple. The key to caring for this beautiful little tree is moisture and warmth.
SITE: Aim for bright light, although this plant will tolerate varying light levels, from low light to full sun.
TEMPERATURE: Average to warm room temperature (65–85°F/18–29°C).
WATERING: Water thoroughly and allow the potting mix to dry out between waterings.
FEEDING: Feed monthly from spring through fall (autumn) with a balanced liquid fertilizer.
TIP: *Cut back on water in the winter when growth has slowed.*

RIGHT: An interesting arrangement for the bathroom, featuring a stunning *Maranta leuconeura* (prayer plant) at the top and *Sansevieria trifasciata* and *Aloe haworthioides* at the bottom

PESTS, DISEASES, AND OTHER PROBLEMS

Plants often react in the same way to adverse conditions, such as pest and disease attacks, a lack of light, or over- and underwatering—with yellow or browning leaves or wilting stems, or by shedding their leaves. Try to work out what the problem may be by asking yourself a few questions: Are you watering correctly? Are you feeding correctly? Does the plant have enough light? Is the pot the right size? The following guide may help you to identify the cause of the problem.

Physiological problems

Yellowing leaves

POSSIBLE CAUSE: Underwatering. When plants are too dry, they cannot take up water, which also contains valuable nutrients.
SOLUTION: Check the potting mix regularly to see if it is dry, and water if necessary.

POSSIBLE CAUSE: Overwatering. Waterlogged roots cannot function and thus are unable to provide the plant with water and nutrients.
SOLUTION: Make sure the pot has ample drainage holes and also that it's not standing in a water-filled saucer.

POSSIBLE CAUSE: Lack of nutrients. Nitrogen is essential to the production of a green pigment called chlorophyll, which harnesses light energy so that the plant can photosynthesize. If a plant is short of nitrogen, the available nitrogen moves to the top of the plant where it's most needed, resulting in the bottom leaves turning yellow.
SOLUTION: Regular feeding.

POSSIBLE CAUSE: Low temperatures. Yellowing leaves may occur if a plant is used to warm temperatures.
SOLUTION: Move the plant to a warmer position.

POSSIBLE CAUSE: Hard water on lime-hating plants, which raises the lime content.
SOLUTION: Use soft water or a feed that is specific to neutralize the lime.

Leaf, flower, or bud drop

POSSIBLE CAUSE: Underwatering. The plant sheds leaves or flowers to conserve moisture.
SOLUTION: Check the potting mix regularly to see if it is dry, and water if necessary.

POSSIBLE CAUSE: Changes in light levels. Leaves can become detached as they adjust to the new light levels.
SOLUTION: Avoid turning the plant dramatically too often.

POSSIBLE CAUSE: Changes in temperature, which can shock the plant.
SOLUTION: Provide stable growing conditions.

Scorched leaves

POSSIBLE CAUSE: Not enough moisture. Leaves lose water faster through transpiration than it can travel up the plant from the roots, so the leaves turn brown at the edges.
SOLUTION: Move the plant to a more humid area.

POSSIBLE CAUSE: Too much heat. Hot conditions such as those found near radiators or from direct sunlight may scorch the plant.
SOLUTION: Move plant to a cooler area.

Pests

Aphids (greenfly)
WHAT TO LOOK FOR: Distorted stems and leaves; damaged flowers; sticky honeydew on plants.
SOLUTION: Rub the insects off or use a biological nematode control.

Leaf rolling caterpillars
WHAT TO LOOK FOR: Nibbled leaves and stems; rolled-up leaves with a fine, sticky webbing holding them together; distorted growth caused by leaves or shoots that are stuck together.
SOLUTION: Pick off the caterpillars with your fingers or use a biological nematode control.

Mealy bug
WHAT TO LOOK FOR: Yellowing leaves; tufts of waxy white wool in leaf axils; honeydew on leaves.
SOLUTION: Dig out the bugs or use a biological nematode control.

Red spider mite
WHAT TO LOOK FOR: Mottled or finely spotted leaves; curled-up leaf edges; a fine, silky webbing on leaves and on the underside of leaf axils.
SOLUTION: Use a biological nematode or chemical control.

Soft scale insects
WHAT TO LOOK FOR: Sticky substance on leaves, which may turn black; waxy brown or yellow encrustations on the underside of the leaves.
SOLUTION: Rub the insects off with your fingers or use a biological nematode control.

Vine weevil (larva)
WHAT TO LOOK FOR: Wilting of the whole plant, even when the potting mixture is moist; roots or tubers eaten away.
SOLUTION: Use a chemical or biological nematode control.

Vine weevil (adult)
WHAT TO LOOK FOR: Crescent-shaped sections eaten out of leaves.
SOLUTION: Pick off the weevils with your fingers or use a chemical control.

Whitefly
WHAT TO LOOK FOR: Sticky honeydew on plants; pure white insects on the underside of leaves.
SOLUTION: Use a biological nematode control.

Diseases

Blackleg
WHAT TO LOOK FOR: Strikes where the stem meets the potting mix (normally when the mix is kept too moist). Leaves turn yellow and the stem turns brown up to 4in (10cm) above the soil.
SOLUTION: Always make sure the potting mix can drain properly by providing adequate drainage holes. You may have to dispose of the plant completely, however, and start again by taking cuttings, as the parent plant will probably not recover. Take the cuttings from the top of the plant and dip the ends in hormone rooting power containing a fungicide before potting up.

Botrytis (gray mold)
WHAT TO LOOK FOR: Fluffy gray mold on half-rotted leaves.
SOLUTION: Spray with a fungicide.

Crown or stem rot
WHAT TO LOOK FOR: Soft, slimy stems; black and brown decayed areas.
SOLUTION: Take cuttings from unaffected areas, and spray with sulphur before repotting. Unfortunately, this rot may be fatal to the parent plant.

Fallen petal mold
WHAT TO LOOK FOR: Fallen petals left on leaves can rot and cause mold.
SOLUTION: Remove damaged leaves.

Powdery mildew
WHAT TO LOOK FOR: Powdery white patches on leaves.
SOLUTION: Pick off affected leaves and spray the plant with a fungicide.

Sooty mold
WHAT TO LOOK FOR: Thick, black, soot-like deposits on leaves and stems, growing on honeydew produced by sap-sucking insects.
SOLUTION: Wash the leaves regularly with a soapy liquid such as diluted dishwashing liquid.

chapter 1

enclosed in glass

One of the many joys of growing house plants is being able to create your own living landscape or miniature garden. Glass vessels are exceptional in allowing you to watch, as well as house, your new living worlds. In this chapter, I have used various glass objects to encase and host an array of wonderful house plants, showing off their full glory. From full-scale terrariums and large glass vases to glass bottles and small wineglasses, let your imagination run riot when thinking of ways to display plant-based creations.

AQUATIC PLANTS

Living in London, I often miss the pond at my parents' house. On a warm summer's day, it's so lovely to look at, watching the different fish and admiring the lush aquatic plants. So, I wanted to re-create this effect indoors. Aquatic plants are very much under-used in plant displays, which is a real shame as there are many different and interesting plants to choose from. In fact, with a little imagination, you can create a real show-stopper! It's also fun to visit an out-of-town garden center to shop for aquatic plants; I always like to feed the fish as well. If you live in the heart of the city in a top-floor apartment with no outdoor space, you could easily become despondent at the lack of access to your own green space. That's why indoor planting is so important: it's about bringing greenery indoors. In this imaginative display, you're not only creating something green, but also making a small indoor pond in a beautiful glass vase.

For this display, I included a beautiful piece of dark-colored bark, which is called bogwood, a selection of water moss balls, which are created by the churning of underwater currents, and an *Echinodorus amazonicus* (Amazon sword plant). This is an aquatic plant that is happy to grow solely in water. I secured the plant in place by stitching it onto the piece of bark with some dark cotton. I still haven't decided whether to add some small fish... (For further advice on aquatic horticulture, see below.)

if you live in the city with no outdoor space, you could easily become despondent at the lack of access to your own green space

aquatic horticulture

❖ Aquatic plants are those that have adapted to living in water or very waterlogged soil. The most common aquatic plants are *Taxiphyllum barbieri* (Java moss), *Bacopa caroliniana* (water hyssop), *Ceratophyllum* (hornwort), *Hydrocotyle leucocephala* (Brazilian pennywort), and *Hygrophila difformis* (water wisteria), all of which can easily be found in aquatic stores.

❖ The plants may be secured in a water display in a number of different ways. For example, in the Aquatic Landscape display on the opposite page, I stitched the plants onto the bark with some dark cotton thread, while for the Zen Aquatic Terrarium on page 66, I simply weighed down the plants with some large pebbles.

❖ If you are growing plants in this way, you will need to change the water regularly, especially when it starts to get murky. I usually add two aspirins to the water in order to aid the plants' growth and prevent a build-up of bacteria. Also, bear in mind that algae growing on tank walls or on plant leaves will compete with the plants for light. You can remove the algae manually by scrubbing or scraping the walls of the tank weekly when you're changing the water, and by rubbing the leaves gently between your fingers.

❖ Another area of aquatic horticulture, often referred to as hydroculture, is the growing of ordinary plants in a soil-less medium or an aquatic-based environment—the plant takes its nutrients from the water. The roots of the plant might be anchored in clay aggregate and pebbles. Plants commonly grown in this way include *Tradescantia fluminensis* "Albovittata" and *Cyperus alternifolius* (umbrella plant), and many bulbs, such as hyacinths.

cacti and succulents—a history

The word "succulent" is a descriptive term given to those plants that store water in their leaves or stems. Cacti belong to a large family of plants that are all succulents. There are also other types of succulent besides cacti. So, as a rule, remember that all cacti are succulents, but not all succulents are cacti. The word "cactus" is derived, through Latin, from the ancient Greek (*kaktos*), a name that was originally used for a spiny plant whose identity is now uncertain. Succulents are found in many countries all over the world and have always held an attraction for gardeners because of their curious and exotic appearance. During the 15th century, the famous Portuguese explorers Bartholomeu Dias (1451–1500) and Vasco da Gama (1460–1524) collected succulents such as *Aloe*, *Haworthia*, *Stapelia*, and many others from Africa. They also discovered *Caralluma* and *Euphorbia* (spurge) in India during exploratory trips to find new trade routes to that country. The Dutch East India Company, which was established in 1602, was also responsible for collecting many succulent species for the Dutch government. Many of these succulents also found their way to the world-famous Royal Botanic Gardens at Kew, in London.

desert plants have always held an **attraction** for gardeners because of their curious and **exotic appearance**

OPPOSITE AND ABOVE When planting a terrarium, try grouping different types of *Echeveria* succulents to make an impact

RIGHT A striking way to display cacti—use pebbles and fossils as a decorative topping to evoke their desert homes

DESERT HEARTH

If you're lucky enough to have an original fireplace, but don't have time to light a regular fire, then this handsome selection of cacti is for you. Of course, you don't need a fireplace to enjoy this display: an empty corner, or perhaps an unnoticed spot by the stairs, would work equally well. This display sits in a selection of beautiful copper lanterns. Rather helpfully, the cacti and succulents are all easy to care for and very low maintenance. They live well regardless of being in the shade and receiving just a little water, making them perfect plants for the novice or occasionally lazy gardener! (For further advice on caring for cacti and succulents, see page 51.)

The striking *Echinocactus grusonii* (golden barrel cactus) in the smaller black lantern is armed with stout golden-yellow spines arranged carefully in rows on ribbed stems; it is quite the attention-seeker. You may find that it's sometimes known as the golden ball or, rather cheekily, as mother-in-law's cushion. I think it is one of the most distinctive of all cacti, and it is often used in architectural gardening owing to its spherical shape.

Planting cacti or succulents in unusual containers is a great way to show off their wonderful shapes

BELOW Left to right: *Mammillaria crinita*, *Echinocactus grusonii*, and *Aloe haworthioides*

handling difficult plants

The following method is a great way to handle prickly plants such as cacti and ones that produce an irritating sap. Take a piece of folded newspaper or cloth, wrap it around the plant, and then use it as a handle while you knock the plant out of the upturned pot. Keep the newspaper in place while you position the plant in its new pot and until you have firmed in some fresh potting mix around the plant. Remove the "handle" once the plant is firmly in place.

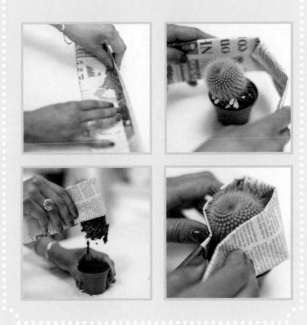

Cacti can often be quite severe plants, but I find that *Mammillaria crinita* (rose pincushion cactus), seen in the larger dark lantern, is absolutely lovely. It's another spherical cactus and is covered in regularly arranged yellow and brown spines. There are numerous reddish-purple flowers, which form a dense ring at the top. Also featured in this display is an *Aloe haworthioides* sitting tightly in a clay pot. This perennial succulent has lush, glossy leaves and small, rosette-like flowers. I also used gravel and reindeer moss in the display, as well as vintage medicine bottles.

CREATING A TERRARIUM

A few simple guidelines should be followed when preparing a terrarium container: it must be made from glass or another clear material through which light can pass; there should be a large enough opening to allow you to add potting mix and plants; and the plants you select should all have similar environmental needs.

The basics of terrarium horticulture are easy. Once you've found a suitable terrarium container, make sure you clean it thoroughly before use to prevent bacteria growing inside. Place some rocks at the bottom for drainage, and add a layer of charcoal and clay pellets. I usually add these using a funnel made from a piece of strong card, as terrariums often have quite small openings. The charcoal and clay pellets are important because they help to reduce excess moisture and the build-up of molds, odors, and fungus, keeping the terrarium environment healthy. This is because the charcoal acts as a purifier: as the water cycles through the terrarium, it is cleansed by the carbon in the charcoal. You can then add the potting mix and, finally, the plants. You may also include a few decorations if you wish. There are lots of different ways to present your indoor garden and make it look extra-special.

1 Put a layer of clay gravel or rocks, about 1¼in (3cm) deep, at the bottom of the terrarium. Add a layer of charcoal and clay pellets, approximately ½–¾in (1–2cm) deep, on top of the clay gravel or rocks.

2 Fill the terrarium with approximately 2–2¼in (5–6cm) of potting mix. Use a mini trowel to smooth out the potting mix and make a hole for each of the plants.

3 Take your chosen plants—in the examples here and on pages 50–51 I have used a mix of small cacti, mosses, and grasses. You can use either a pair of long-handled tweezers or a fork to position the plants in their holes. Firm down the plants to anchor them securely in the potting mix. Pat down the exposed potting mix with a flat-topped fork.

4 If you are using moss, take some sheet moss and break off a piece to the size needed to cover the exposed potting mix. Using the flat-topped fork, gently firm down the moss.

5 Use a spray bottle to water the terrarium. It's best to spray, rather than use a watering can, because terrarium plants tend to be delicate. Spraying will also help to increase humidity levels, which the plants love.

6 Use a long-handled sponge to clean any dirt and debris from the sides of the terrarium.

7 Use a brush to remove any stray specks of potting mix and ensure your terrarium is spotlessly clean.

caring for cacti and succulents

Desert cacti and succulents like a warm, sunny location where they will receive around four to six hours of warm sunlight every day. Place cacti in the sunniest spot in your home, perhaps on a windowsill or a table close to a window. Please note that forest cacti, such as *Schlumbergera* (Christmas cactus), will need some shade and less intense heat than desert cacti in summer, as well as a potting mix rich in organic matter and a little humidity.

❖ **Potting mix:** Use a potting mix specially formulated for cacti and succulents with added gravel and sand.

❖ **Watering:** Water cacti and succulents as needed—about once a month. A good indication that your cacti need watering is to lift the pot and see how heavy it is. If the pot feels lighter than usual, it's time to water your plant.

❖ **Feeding:** Feed cacti with a house plant fertilizer that is high in nitrates and phosphorus. Feed once or twice a year, diluting the fertilizer to half the manufacturer's recommended amount.

❖ **Handling cacti:** Always use a strip of newspaper or card when handling cacti to avoid pricking your fingers (see page 47).

OPPOSITE Soft and bright "cushion moss" is lovely viewed from all sides of this angular terrarium

TOP RIGHT Keep the humidity level in your terrarium constant by adding pebbles and misting regularly with water

RIGHT The small, abundant leaves of a *Portulacaria afra* (miniature jade plant) look like tiny jewels in this display

this champagne flute terrarium *is another example of how thinking* imaginatively *can be so successful when you are* designing *a terrarium display*

TEXTURED AND COLORFUL

This display is a wonderful example of how different textures and colors can work exceptionally well together. The delicate glass of the tall flute is offset beautifully by the weathered terracotta pot. You wouldn't automatically expect it, but the glass and pot work very well next to each other. This champagne flute terrarium is another example of how thinking imaginatively can be so successful when you are designing a terrarium display. Terrariums need not be vintage cases or steel-framed boxes—a dramatically shaped glass vase such as this will provide a beautiful home for your plants.

The bright yellow flowers of *Craspedia globosa* (bachelor's buttons) are akin to champagne bubbles floating to the top of a glass. They are bright and glossy, and just a few here and there create a wonderful picture; too many of them would be overkill.

Alongside the bachelor's buttons, I used a mossy green *Selaginella apoda* and a purple-flowered *Passiflora* (passionflower) to provide a lush green backdrop for the yellow flowers and brown bark. You will need to keep the passionflower trimmed back as it grows so that it doesn't swamp the container.

In the antique terracotta pot, I planted peach-colored Tom Thumb (a hybrid of *Kalanchoe blossfeldiana*), which is a lovely brightly colored plant that matches the weather-worn orange clay pot.

WINEGLASS SUCCULENTS

These three differently shaped wineglasses are perfect for bringing added interest to the display on the previous page. Here, I used a mix of different succulents, as well as some bun moss, to create a little world of interest. You can place a few pebbles in the base of the glasses to provide extra drainage, but as long as you remember that these plants don't require lots of water, they should be fine. I have not included any potting mix here, but the succulents should last as long as the moss is kept moist.

VICTORIAN TERRARIUM

This handsome assortment of dark bark and pale pebbles makes an arresting display for any corner of a room. The dark tones in the vintage terrarium remind me of a dark-hued Victorian gentleman's club from the 19th century, containing collected finds from a desert expedition. I discovered this terrarium in an antiques market and, after some polishing and careful cleaning, it looks new once more. The plants in the terrarium are *Tillandsia*, or air plants. (For further advice on how to grow and care for air plants, see page 104.)

To complete the scene, I added an interestingly shaped piece of wood and some reindeer moss, and then scattered the base of the terrarium with bark chips and a few pebbles.

This is one of my favorite terrarium displays, as it's very simple and elegant, while still having an air of luxury. The background and surroundings are so unassuming that they really allow the air plants to shine and stand out in all their regal exquisiteness. Encased in such a wonderful terrarium, these air plants would look just as good with only the bogwood as a simple pedestal.

these **wonderfully** exotic air plants call for **careful** scrutiny. Arranged with some wood and moss, this **combination** is a real show-stopper

terrariums—a brief history

In 1827, a London doctor called Nathaniel Ward created a terrarium by accident while building a fern rockery. Ward found that his plants kept dying because of poisoning by heavy fumes from London's factories. He was also studying moths and caterpillars, keeping several insects in covered jars so that he could observe their behavior. Ward placed several plants, including some of the rockery ferns, alongside the cocoons. He noticed that the plants were healthy and grew well in the warm conditions under the enclosed glass, and came to the conclusion that plants could flourish in London if protected from the city's polluted air.

Ward spent years experimenting with miniature greenhouses and planting indoors, and eventually developed the Wardian case or terrarium. It was an exciting discovery for horticulturalists who were able to bring back sensitive tropical plants in Wardian cases that kept them well protected from salty air and changing climatic conditions during long sea voyages. Wardian cases became popular with fashionable households, and it became trendy to keep one in your front room. They grew into miniature Taj Mahals and Brighton Pavilions, and were a wonderful way for Victorians to display decorative objects beside living plants.

delicate **shades** of pink and red serve
to **enhance** the arrangements in
this **traditional** glasshouse

LAYERED TERRARIUM

This large terrarium (shown opposite) needs plenty of space. It's quite an eye-catcher, being a heady combination of color and texture. The traditional shape and form of the terrarium remind me of a Victorian garden room—very structured with large panes of glass. Here, I've gone for a complete contrast in the planting. Indeed, instead of adhering to clear lines and color blocks, as the shape of the terrarium would suggest, I've created layers of moss and succulents, below the darker *Begonia* and *Fittonia* (nerve plant). It reminds me of a secret garden hidden on a country estate away from prying eyes.

BELOW This terrarium called for a single plant with strong colors. I chose this lovely *Callistemon* (bottlebrush plant), with its striking bright pink flowers, which I knew would be just right for this majestic house. This is a very striking terrarium, and an arrangement such as this needs attention and pride of place in your home

CARNIVOROUS COCKTAIL

Cocktails on a Friday night are always something to look forward to after a particularly long, tiring week. This fun and flirty display is a celebration of the cocktail. It's a heady mix of both color and structure, and—like all good cocktails—it is a real attention-grabber. You can't be nervous about this plant display; it needs to be put in a prominent position for all to admire.

Rather wonderfully, the tall plants in the center of the vase are a type of pitcher plant called *Sarracenia leucophylla*, which, for me, is a comical reminder of those sugary cocktails served in large pitchers. Not so here, however. In this display, the pitcher plants are elegant and sculptural. Be aware, though, that pitcher plants are carnivorous, featuring a deep cavity filled with liquid, which is known as a pitfall trap, for capturing hapless insects. Although this may sound ominous, plants as small as those pictured are dormant and pose no risk (yet!) to passing flies.

Pitcher plants prefer boggy, humid environments, so make sure the potting mix remains constantly moist. Rather than using tap water, it's advisable to use distilled water or rainwater, or perhaps water collected from condensation, even from an air-conditioner or dehumidifier. I also recommend planting pitcher plants in a soil-less potting mix, combining one part peat-substitute with one part sterilized sand. I put a layer of bark chips on top of the potting mix to help retain moisture. Pitcher plants also need plenty of sun, so be sure to place them in an area that receives at least six hours of direct sunlight each day in summer.

Surrounding the pitcher plants are handsome *Viola* x *wittrockiana* (pansies), pretty little flowers, which, in this case, are a beautiful deep color. Pansies are a large group of plants that are the result of a cross between two wild violets, and are said to attract love! They are available in many colors.

this glass container is striking in its majestic beauty. Standing tall and proud, it is an effortlessly chic arrangement that hints at delicious cocktail flavors

gloriously green in color, this **stunning** glass terrarium can be set off by a wonderful array of **ferns** to create a **lush** landscape

FERN TERRARIUM

This striking, thick green glass dome makes a wonderful house for a plant display (opposite). The narrow neck and thick glass keep the heat inside the dome—if using a terrarium made from thick glass, bear this in mind and select plants that thrive in warm, moist conditions. The dark soil here is a great base for the green moss, *Fittonia* (nerve plant), and array of ferns.

I found this carboy terrarium in a small craft shop and was immediately drawn to it, as I remember my mother having one when I was small. They were very popular in the 1970s, and many came with a large cork stopper to seal the top of the terrarium. It's very different from all the other terrariums in my collection and I just loved its simple, curved lines.

The Boston fern and *Fittonia* create lots of interesting textures, which can be glimpsed through the wonderful green glass. This is a lovely, simple terrarium that boasts a warm, rustic feel.

STONES AND CACTI TERRARIUMS

This handsome trio of glass terrariums features an eclectic selection of different cacti, stones, and green mosses. Cacti hark back to an open, desert landscape—the final frontier. Here, they are captured in three beautiful open glass vases. (For further advice on caring for cacti and succulents, see page 51.)

Attractive glass vases are easy to get from homeware stores, but it's a good idea to shop around to find vases that you particularly like and which will work in your indoor space. Think about where you want to put them, how much space you have, and how much light the space receives.

The three vases pictured here are all different shapes and sizes, but still work well as a single display. Don't be afraid of placing terrariums and vases next to each other. Inside the vases is a selection of different pebbles that I collected from walks on the beach. Try to choose pebbles with different colors and textures that will contrast well. Pretty shells can also look striking in glass displays. If fact, picking up shells and pebbles that can be used

Let your imagination run wild with glass pots and vases of different shapes and sizes—anything goes!

in a vase or terrarium once you return home can be a fun family vacation activity. I also found some pieces of granite and dried moss, which I used in the display to create different pockets of interest.

In the cylindrical vase, I used floristry sheet moss, which is lined with paper, making it easier to cut and shape to fit inside containers. This lush green moss looks wonderful, its lovely, bright, solid color creating a great juxtaposition with the desert-like appearance of the other vases. The accents of fossils and small *Lithops* (living stones or stone plants) are a nod to archeological discovery. Finally, I added a beautiful green gemstone to represent a blue pond surrounded by glistening rocks.

ABOVE Playful decorations like this beautiful green gemstone add an individual touch to terrariums

ZEN AQUATIC TERRARIUM

This small water garden (opposite) is weighed down with large pebbles and rocks, which remind me of a rugged coastline. Indeed, I collected many of these stones on a recent trip to the Cornish coast. Looking after my terrariums has turned me into something of a magpie; I'm always looking for little objects that can be used in a project. In an aquatic store, I was inspired to buy a couple of different green water plants, namely *Myriophyllum* (water milfoil) and *Alternanthera*, which I knew would look lovely against the ashen color of the stones. The pretty clematis flower was picked from the garden to decorate the scene; it looks like a cool blue water lily floating on the surface of the water. (For further advice on aquatic horticulture, see page 43.)

water-themed containers are guaranteed to bring peace and serenity to all those who gaze on them

In the glass container shown opposite I used *Fittonia argyroneura*, *Echinodorus* "Red Special," and an aquatic fern. I weighed down the plants using pebbles. This glorious red-hued display creates a very sophisticated look on the mantelpiece

old finds

Using unexpected objects as containers, as well as recycling old ones, is a wonderfully inventive way to show off and exhibit house plants. Here, I have collected a wealth of unusual containers to hold botanical displays. From old pots to milk jugs and pitchers, there is always a way to update and recycle unwanted objects. The most rewarding aspect of using old finds for plant displays is the search—I love nothing better than trawling through antiques markets or thrift stores, hunting for suitable containers. With a little effort, you can easily bring them up to scratch and create a truly unique spectacle.

TROPICAL BATHROOM

A long soak in the tub is a wonderful opportunity for some "me" time in a busy life, but I think bathrooms are all too often neglected spaces for indoor plants. It's a great shame to see a single plant sitting by itself in the corner, or even no greenery at all! However, bathrooms make wonderful backdrops for indoor plants, as they are often flooded with light and the bright spaces allow the plants to shine.

The succulents and bright, fleshy plants in this wonderfully dark arrangement all thrive in the warm surroundings of a bathroom. These plants also all retain moisture well and boast a beautiful depth of color.

One of my favorites is the tall *Maranta leuconeura* (prayer plant), with its stunning combination of colors that are set off by the dark clay pot. The patterns and coloring of this plant's leaves easily make it one of the most attractive plants in any arrangement you might put together. I have also discovered that the leaves of prayer plants partially fold up at night, just like hands at prayer!

The dark green *Aloe haworthioides* is a really luxuriant plant with its spiky, fleshy leaves. It is a great plant for a bathroom and easily grows in full sun to partial shade. It flowers in late summer and early fall (autumn) and has beautifully delicate apricot blooms with a deliciously sweet fragrance. *Aloe haworthioides* is named for the resemblance to its cousins in the genus *Haworthia*. This resemblance is not a coincidence: *Aloe* and *Haworthia* are genetically close ,and they hybridize easily.

You should be careful for whom you buy the comically named mother-in-law's tongue! It is perhaps more diplomatic to call it by its botanical name—*Sansevieria trifasciata*. This is a dense, succulent perennial with stiff, sharp, evergreen leaves.

a **stunning** combination of different **leaf shapes** and colors really makes this bathroom arrangement **stand out** from the crowd

BOWLFUL OF SUCCULENTS

This stylish display is a must for the "I wish I had more time!" gardener, the "I always forget to water the plants" gardener, or simply the lazy gardener. In recent years, succulents have come out of the shadows and they can be seen regularly on the tables of trendy cafes and in the pages of hip interior design magazines.

The odd shapes, the fleshy leaves, and the sculptural globes make very modern and stylish interior plants. They are minimalist, with simple, streamlined shapes, and easily add a "desert chic" look to any home.

It can be a lot of fun putting together a display of succulents—you can definitely include the weird

and the wonderful here. I chose a selection of my favorites, including *Crassula ovata* (jade or money plant), *Sempervivum tectorum* (common house-leek or hens-and-chicks), *Aloe* "Pinto," *Sedum*, *Kalanchoe thyrsiflora* (paddle plant), *Epipremnum aureum* (devil's ivy), *Echeveria* "Fred Ives," *Crassula perforata* (string of buttons), and *Pachyveria glauca* "Little Jewel," along with *Lithops* (living stones or stone plant) and neutral pebbles. I painted the bowl a dark slate color, which I think offsets the overall look very well. (For further advice on caring for succulents, see page 51.)

the intricate beauty and delicacy of these fantastic succulent plants are set off to perfection by the surrounding stones

HEART FERN CONTAINER

Deep orange terracotta reminds me of vacations in Spain or Greece—as soon as you glance at the rich clay of a terracotta pot, you're instantly transported to sunny climes with the vacation sun shining on your face. This striking globe-like terracotta pot makes a wonderfully simple container for *Hemionitis arifolia* (heart fern), a glossy green plant with heart-shaped leaves. Heart ferns grow to 6in (15cm) in height, making them perfect for growing in terrariums. They need shade and a well-drained potting mix.

a delicate
heart-shaped
fern is enhanced
wonderfully
by the warmth
of the small
terracotta
vessel

COLORFUL PAINTED POTS

Neon colors are startling and fresh in the modern home. An instant hit of color automatically lifts any interior—and is perfect for a white-toned home. I chose two solid, round zinc planters and carefully painted a neon-red strip around the top with paint bought at my local craft store.

I then chose two green succulents (*Aeonium* "Dinner Plate" and *Crassula*) and planted them in the center of the pots. It's a simple, easy-to-create look, but one that boasts both style and an injection of color.

I love the simplicity of this project. Using plants with different forms, but with the same color tone, will allow them to shine. One of the most interesting features of this display, along with the unusual textures and shapes, is the juxtaposition between the fresh green of the plants and the vibrant orange of the pots. This is an aesthetic treat for the eyes, I am sure you'll agree.

a striking way to set your plant displays apart is to add a splash of color by painting the containers

is there a better or more **rewarding** way to enhance your **cooking** than by using freshly picked **herbs**, such as rosemary and thyme, that you have grown **yourself**?

FRENCH HERB CONTAINER

What could be more satisfying than reaching over and picking some fresh, home-grown rosemary to use with your Sunday roast lamb?

Parisians and other apartment dwellers living in mainland European cities are often starved of outdoor space, so they make the most of their balconies and indoor planting areas. Walking through the streets of Paris and looking up to the sky, you will often see apartments lined with window boxes and lushly planted balconies. Parisians love to grow their own herbs and produce to use in cooking, and don't see a lack of outdoor space as a hindrance. I picked up this French wooden crate at an antiques market and particularly liked the markings of the Mondot Saint-Émilion wine —a good vintage, I've been told! The rustic-looking crate is perfect for the herbs housed inside, creating a picturesque miniature French herb garden.

You can often find wooden crates in vintage and antiques stores; sometimes, you might spot a neglected one at the back of the store, containing other bits and pieces—they're often cheap and you can haggle with the seller!

The compact thyme bushes look great in this crate. Thyme can be grown successfully indoors; it simply needs a bright windowsill and some basic care and attention to thrive. The heady scent emanating from rosemary is delicious, and this highly fragrant herb can be used in many dishes. It is very easy to grow and, being a Mediterranean herb, it will appreciate a sunny spot. Finally, the lavender plant makes a lovely partner for both the thyme and the rosemary. Lavender is hard to resist, boasting beautiful flowers and an equally arresting scent. It gives a delicate flavor to cooking and is especially wonderful in light desserts.

CUTTING FRESH FLOWERS FOR DISPLAY

This vintage wooden container with its antique glass bottles makes a really striking indoor (or outdoor) floral display. I found these objects in a flea market, but you could also use milk bottles and any wooden fruit crate. The finished project appears on page 136.

1 Choose a simple posy of long-stemmed flowers for each bottle. I prefer a mix of meadow flowers in pastel colors.

2 Here, I used *Craspedia globosa* (bachelor's buttons), *Scabiosa* (scabious), *Mentha* (mint), *Centaurea cyanus* (cornflower), *Delphinium* (larkspur), *Lisianthus* (also called *Eustoma*), and *Anthriscus sylvestris* (cow parsley).

3 Hold the stems up to the base of a bottle and cut them to size. I find that stems of slightly different lengths look more natural.

4 For most plants, you will only need to make a diagonal cut at the bottom of the stem, but you should also snip the bottom of the stem of tougher plants in the middle to increase the take-up of water. Mix the posies of flowers, using three or four different colors in each bottle, to create a vintage look.

SUMMER FLORAL ARRANGEMENT

Flower-arranging is often regarded as a rather staid and old-fashioned hobby. However, there has recently been a noticeable resurgence in floral arrangements, with edgier displays featuring wilder flowers that are markedly different from commercial blooms. This bountiful floral display, which includes roses, peonies, delphiniums, *Salvia farinacea* (ornamental sage), *Chamelaucium uncinatum* (Geraldton waxflower), and *Brodiaea* (cluster lilies), is bright and colorful, and housed perfectly in a white kitchen jug. The eclectic mix of color and foliage makes for a lovely contrast with the pale hues of the open kitchen. Flower-arranging is a wonderful pastime; I love whiling away an afternoon arranging my favorite flowers—it's a creative, rewarding, and therapeutic activity.

CALLA LILLIES AND DAHLIA

The deep gray of this pot creates a very attractive container for the startlingly vibrant flowers inside. To produce this effect, I painted a terracotta pot with my favorite shade of eggshell paint—a dark, moody gray. For the planting, I used *Zantedeschia* "Picasso" calla lilies and *Dahlia* "Violet". This display isn't merely for decoration, however:

it provides a real opportunity to be an indoor gardener, tending to the leaves and flowers. The storm-cloud-gray pot emphasizes the flowers, creating a wonderful display for a dull spot.

luscious shades of purple, from the plum-purple of the calla lilies to the fuchsia-pink of the dahlias, produce a magnificent pageant of color.

BONSAI DISPLAY

Sometimes smaller can be better. The joy of indoor planting is filling a bare spot in your home or adding some green to a favorite arrangement of pictures or ornaments. This eclectic group of small Eastern-inspired plantings looks perfect next to a few empty vintage bottles and some bright signage.

People often think of bonsai as rather staid and overdone indoor plants, but they look clean and fresh in a simple arrangement such as this. This specimen is called *Serissa foetida* (also known as *S. japonica*, tree of a thousand stars). Growing and pruning miniature bonsai trees is an ancient tradition, passed down through generations of Chinese and then Japanese gardeners. Their popularity in the West grew with the growth of foreign travel, and they soon became absorbed into everyday interiors. This simple look brings them into the 21st century. (For advice on caring for bonsai, see overleaf.)

Next to the bonsai plant is a stem of *Dracaena sanderiana* (lucky bamboo). Lucky bamboo is happy to grow without any potting mix in only a few inches of water. It prefers moderate or indirect light; it is best to avoid direct sun, which will scorch the leaves. Replenish the vase with fresh water every 7–10 days. Feeding every 3–4 weeks with a drop of liquid fertilizer is sufficient.

Dracaena sanderiana (lucky bamboo) is happy to grow in only a few inches of water, making it a brilliant plant for impromptu displays

caring for bonsai

Caring well for a bonsai specimen is very important if you are to keep it healthy. Place the tree in a light position, but not in direct sunlight as this will speed up evaporation and dry the plant out. Like most house plants, bonsai plants don't like being placed near a heat source such as a radiator, or in drafty places. Here are a few guidelines on bonsai care:

❖ *Watering:* This is very important, as the potting mix needs to be kept moist at all times—you'll need to check the surface of the potting mix every day because you don't want it to dry out. The best way is to immerse the pot in water until the air bubbles stop rising and then let the water drain away, or you can pour any excess water from the pot.

❖ *Feeding:* Feed your bonsai with a low-nitrogen fertilizer roughly every two weeks between early spring and mid-fall (autumn). Remember to water before feeding.

❖ *Pruning:* You'll need to prune your bonsai regularly to maintain its shape. When a branch grows to about six to eight leaves, trim it back to about two or three leaves. This will encourage the tree to fill out.

❖ *Wiring:* Wiring your bonsai will enable you to bend and twist the branches into the shape you wish.

❖ *Root pruning and repotting:* This is needed for established bonsai every two or three years in spring, so that you can replenish the potting mix. Remove the plant from the pot and trim the roots to about half their original size with root-clippers. Then repot the bonsai in the same pot with fresh potting mix. This will ensure the tree does not get any bigger.

OPULENT ORCHIDS

Orchids are the most elegant of flowers: a sign of love, beauty, luxury, and strength. Here, the long, graceful sprays of flowers produce a lovely assortment of colors and patterns. Although they typically have white flowers, I opted for a selection of *Phalaenopsis* (moth orchids) with colorful petals to create a fabulously bright picture. I chose subtle mauve and gray ceramic containers for these graceful flowers, creating a perfect contrast with the wonderfully distressed, hand-painted wallpaper that frames the display. (For advice on caring for orchids, see overleaf.)

nothing brings as much elegance and exquisiteness to your home as the astonishingly beautiful flowers of orchids

caring for orchids

Orchids have long been a symbol of love and beauty. The single most important variable when growing orchids indoors is light levels. Most orchids prefer bright, indirect light. Orchids also thrive in a variety of different temperatures, so choose the best position in your house to suit the needs of the particular orchid you are growing.

❖ *Watering and misting:* Orchids like high levels of humidity and should be watered once a week with tepid water. Their roots will rot in wet potting mix, so tip out any excess water. Mist the foliage and aerial roots daily, or increase the humidity by standing the orchid pot in a large saucer covered with pebbles, filling the saucer with water to just below the top of the pebbles.

❖ *Feeding:* Feed orchids every three weeks with a specialist orchid fertilizer. They will need a period of rest in winter, so don't feed them during this time.

❖ *Flowering:* Placing orchids outdoors in the summer months may help promote flowering.

PALM ROOM DIVIDER

Vintage industrial containers make the perfect planters for a large plant display. A discarded steel bath or large box can be used to create a cool urban look for your plants. I found this particular planter at my favorite antiques market, and I believe it's originally from the United States. Those "in the know" arrive early at the market for the best finds and bargains. After befriending a few of the sellers, I bagged a number of old industrial containers for planting. It's important to give containers such as these a good wash, and to provide a good layer of drainage in the base (but don't drill holes in the bottom of the planter unless it will be placed outside). The lush green plant is *Howea forsteriana* (Kentia palm), which is tall and needs a solid planter. I finished off the display by adding a decorative mulch of pale beach pebbles. Here, the plant also works as a room divider, a green wall creating a small home office in the corner of a living room.

MASON JAR CONTAINERS

These three vintage preserving jars are perfect for a kitchen display of indoor plants. Terrarium-style planters need not be expensive, since the plants don't need to be housed in antique cases or terrariums commissioned from a specialist maker. In fact, it's more fun to think outside the box and be imaginative. So, visit antiques stores, flower markets, and thrift stores, or look in your own home—are there any jars or vases that you've always kept but never found a use for?

I found these beautiful matching vintage jars while in the United States. They were produced during the 1920s and 1930s. As soon as I spotted them, I knew they would look great in my kitchen.

When I found the jars I was on vacation close to the coast, so I have kept that lovely feeling and can remind myself of walks on the beach by using golden sand as a base for the plants. Succulents grow very well in sand; simply place a spoonful or two of succulent potting mix in the base of the jar, then sprinkle the sand around the sides and over the top to hide the potting mix. I used reindeer moss in all three jars and picked different glossy succulents, including *Crassula ovata* (jade or money plant), which is one of my favorites. Other succulents you could use include *Schlumbergera* (Christmas cactus), *Sempervivum tectorum* (common houseleek or, rather charmingly, hens-and-chicks), and *Kalanchoe tomentosa* (panda plant). Spend some time looking into your preferred succulents and thinking about which colors would work best in your own kitchen. Water your succulents sparingly.

preserve special memories of vacations by the sea by keeping found objects in beautiful mason jars

a fun and
inventive way
of using old light bulbs
in order to display
seasonal cuttings
from the *garden*

UNUSUAL IDEAS

For this arrangement I turned to a spot of do-it-yourself and repurposed some old light bulbs that I was storing under the stairs. After the light bulbs had gathered dust for a few months, I had a flash of interior inspiration after visiting an art exhibition in Stockholm and spotting some empty light bulbs in a stunning display. I knew the stark and industrial-looking light bulbs would make perfect modern, miniature terrariums; they also make a great contrast to the natural elements in the display. There are various ways to turn the light bulbs into miniature terrariums, and these techniques can all be found online. It is rather fiddly, but I think well worth it. I used a plumbing ring, which I glued onto the base of each light bulb, to add stability.

The light bulbs make wonderful holders for cuttings and the stems of plants such as the white *Syringa vulgaris* (lilac) featured here. I also used white roses, a variegated variety of *Schefflera* (umbrella tree), and *Ficus benjamina* (weeping fig). You don't need to be too exact when choosing cuttings for display, and can take anything from your garden that's in flower or looking attractive. Just aim to include a mix that you enjoy looking at. The light-bulb-factory look makes a great modern contrast to any overly pretty plants and flowers. It's also effective to mis-match the sizes of the light bulbs and the various cuttings.

ferns—a history

Ferns have been growing on Earth for more than 360 million years. In that time, their diversification into lots of different forms has been truly astonishing. Ferns grow in a wide variety of habitats around the world. They first appear in the fossil records of the early Carboniferous Period, and by the Triassic Period, there is the first evidence of ferns related to several modern fern families. The "great fern radiation," a time when many modern families of ferns first appeared, occurred in the late Cretaceous Period. This period is often referred to as the Age of Ferns, because they were such a dominant feature of the vegetation at that time.

During this era, some fern-like groups—known as seed ferns—evolved from seeds, making up perhaps half of the fern-like foliage of the Carboniferous forests and much later giving rise to flowering plants. Most of the ferns of the Carboniferous Period became extinct, but some later evolved into our modern ferns. There are about 12,000 species of fern in the world today.

Ferns are not of major economic importance, but they can be grown or gathered for food, kept as ornamental plants in the home, and used for treating contaminated soils. They have also been the subjects of research into their ability to remove certain chemical pollutants from the air. For example, they can be used to remove pollutants such as toluene and xylene, which are found in certain paints, nail polishes, and glues.

Ferns also play a significant role in mythology, medicine, and art. Called *koru* in Maori, they are a popular motif in New Zealand.

OPPOSITE A stunning "living wall," featuring *Heuchera micrantha* (midnight rose), *Adiantum* (maidenhair fern), and *Dryopteris filix-mas* "Linearis Polydactyla"

ABOVE, RIGHT The delicate leaves of the maidenhair fern are called "pinnae"

RIGHT *Nephrolepis exaltata* (Boston or sword fern) is easy to care for and a natural humidifier

ferns have been
growing
on Earth for
more than
360 million
years

DECORATIVE MOSS

Walking down the high street in Hampstead, north London, one day, I was struck by a scene in one of the store windows. Here lay a luscious carpet of moss and some cloches containing shoes. This got me thinking: why not have such "scenes" in your home? House plants don't need to be kept in traditional containers, and you can definitely have fun creating scenes with different themes. I really love this particular display, as it's a real show-stopper that reminds me of a mysterious woodland landscape. It would also be a lovely way to showcase your house plants when you have friends over for dinner, or just to please yourself.

To create the scene, I laid a lush carpet of mosses, using a mixture of bun, reindeer, and sheet moss, which I then interspersed with succulents to provide additional texture and interest. I used a variety of succulents here, including *Sempervivum tectorum* (common houseleek or hens-and-chicks), *Echeveria elegans* (Mexican snowball), *Anacampseros rufescens*, *Jovibarba hirta* "Andreas Smits", and *Echeveria* "Imbricata", but any can be used for this display. The pieces of driftwood create a wonderfully earthy feel and are further enhanced by shells and more clumps of

moss. The fireplace is the perfect spot for the display, while the glass cloches, housing tiny terracotta pots planted with more moss, create an air of illusion and mystery, suggesting that you may find hidden treasures nearby.

I also used three different kinds of fern, including *Dryopteris filix-mas* "Linearis Polydactyla," a type of hardy fern, and a species of *Adiantum* (maidenhair fern), both of which I placed within the moss carpet. I put a *Cheilanthes lanosa* (hairy lip fern) in the fireplace. These ferns all add height and create the illusion of a forest—texture is really important in this display. As house plants, ferns make

BELOW Create textural interest and height by mixing different varieties of fern within your moss display

OPPOSITE Small mosses look like precious jewels when set under these lovely colored glass cloches

great air purifiers. They also bring a real "Jurassic Park" feel to this display. There are endless ways in which to embellish the scene, so let your imagination run riot and create your own secret garden.

Please note that this scene isn't a "forever" display, but you could contain the moss in trays, ensuring you water them regularly, if you wish to keep it for a couple of months.

tips on growing moss

❖ It is possible to grow moss on a tray. Take some samples of moss from roofs and pavements. Divide the moss into squares measuring approximately 1½–2in (4–5cm), and place these pieces on a layer of well-watered potting mix. Moss takes quite a while to grow, but growing your own means you can use different types that aren't readily available from floristry suppliers.

❖ Soak the moss well with water. It can be stored in the refrigerator or freezer if you don't need to use it all at once.

❖ Mosses need to be kept moist at all times if they are to grow and retain their lush green color.

chapter 3

hanging gardens

I love the idea of hanging plants indoors, because you can really use your ingenuity and creativity here. In many ways, a hanging display also functions as a work of art because you are creating a stunning focal point in your home to show off your house plants. Here, I have used a variety of hanging objects, from macramé pot-holders to metal hanging baskets—there really are no limitations to how you suspend your plants. Two of my favorite projects use simple picture frames to house a selection of mosses and succulents or to display air plants in an easy-to-build pink frame.

HANGING BASKETS

Hanging planters are a wonderful way to display plants indoors, especially if you're short of space. They make a great focal point, particularly hung over a table or kitchen work surface, as well as being a good spot for keeping herbs and other edible plants. The wooden struts of these containers are clean and almost Japanese in their simplicity. They don't distract the eye from the main display on the table and also accentuate the clean lines of the kitchen. The plants, *Coleus* "Wizard Jade" and *Vinca minor* "Variegata" (variegated periwinkle), were planted first in plastic pots before being placed inside the wooden containers. One of the ways in which I like to use plants in the home is by placing them in an unusual position or to replace common household objects. So, here, where you would usually expect to see two lamps hanging above the table, I have used these hanging baskets instead. Not only is this a really interesting way to display plants, but it also adds a lovely and unique touch to a dining setting.

The wonderful thing about this idea is that you can also ring the changes to reflect the different plants in season, as well as to alter the style or effect you wish to create for a particular dining experience.

filled with
variegated foliage and
cool-blue flowers,
these planters are a
delightful way
of enhancing
your dining experience
and table display

air plants

Tillandsia is a genus of around 540 species of evergreen, perennial, flowering air plants in the family *Bromeliaceae*. They are native to the forests, mountains, and deserts of Central and South America, the southern United States, and the West Indies.

The genus *Tillandsia* was named by Carolus Linnaeus (1707–1778), the Swedish botanist, physician, and zoologist who is considered to have laid the foundations of the biological naming scheme known as binomial nomenclature. He is regarded as the father of modern taxonomy and also one of the fathers of modern ecology. Linnaeus named the air plants after the Swedish-born physician and botanist Dr. Elias Tillandz (1640–1693), who lived in Finland and wrote that country's first botanical work. As a doctor, he also prepared medicines for his patients by drawing on his wide-ranging knowledge of plants.

Most air plants are epiphytes, which are plants that grow non-parasitically on another plant, such as a tree. They derive their moisture and nutrients from the air and rain, and also sometimes from any debris that accumulates around them. The roots are used only as anchors.

You can easily attach air plants to bark, as in the Victorian Terrarium (page 56) and Pretty in Pink (overleaf). To do this, I use a waterproof adhesive, although you can also use a hot glue gun if you have one; it is by far the fastest method. It is quite safe to attach the air plants to the bark after the glue has cooled for a few seconds. The plants can be mounted at any time of the year and the roots will grow when conditions are optimum—ideally, warm with high humidity. Mist your air plants regularly with water in order to keep humidity levels high.

air plants
are anchored
to or perch on another
plant or structure,
absorbing
water and nutrients
from air moisture, dew,
and rainwater through
their leaves

air plants require very little water; you just have to **remember** to *mist* them once a week

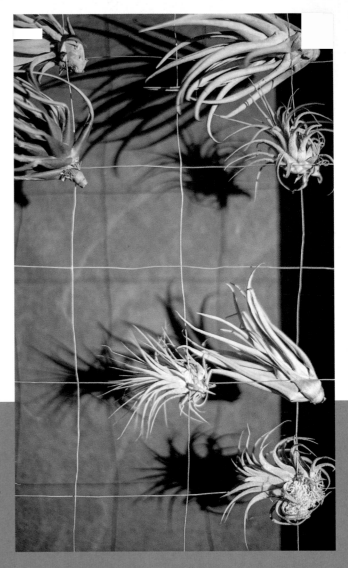

FRAMED
AIR PLANTS

I just love the neon pink here—it is such a luminous and bright color that it automatically draws your attention to the display. It also sits well against the dark gray of the walls, creating a wonderful contrast. I've chosen an array of air plants for this display. Air plants really fascinate me; I think they look great against the bright color of the frame. They require little, if any, water and can hang happily against your wall. You just have to mist them with water once a week.

I attached the air plants to the wires with a hot glue gun. The frame is also fairly easy to construct by drilling holes around the edges to loop the wire through. (For further advice on how to grow and care for air plants, see previous page.)

HANGING BUTTON FERN

Hanging baskets can seem staid and fussy, with too many plants crowded into a small, often ugly basket. This beautiful metallic container breaks the rule, however, as it's both handsome and simple—great for a stylish bedroom or perhaps displayed at the top of a flight of stairs. The delicate, glossy leaves of the plant tumble over the edge of the container, making for an easy, uncluttered look. In this display, I used *Pellaea rotundifolia*, which is commonly known as the button fern. A small, low-growing fern, it is easy to grow and creates a unique look with its small, rounded leaflets.

how wonderful to wake up to the sight of pretty leaves tumbling over the edges of a suspended glass container

the lush **greens and purples** of the plants dripping out of the bottles work really well in a kitchen

HANGING **BOTTLES**

For this creative project, I selected a trio of green-glass wine bottles. Recycling and reusing containers is a wonderful way to make the most of budget gardening. You really don't need very much—just some ingenuity to create a lovely green picture.

The lush greens and purples of the plants dripping out of the bottles work really well in a kitchen. They look great in any window, but particularly against the steel-framed window here, which is a lovely feature of this kitchen's pantry. The plants used are *Begonia foliosa* (fern begonia), *Hatiora salicornioides* (dancing bones cactus), and *Ficus benjamina* (weeping fig).

GROWING PLANTS IN A HANGING BOTTLE

I really enjoy reusing objects, and this is a wonderful way to convert old wine bottles into a lovely plant display. I love the look of the dark green glass with the purple and green leaves. Once the plants are firmly fixed in the bottles, you will need to water them once a week. To do this, carefully pour a steady stream of water through the neck of the bottle to dampen the potting mix and moss.

1 To create a hanging bottle, carefully score the bottle with a bottle cutter. (It is advisable to wear protective gloves and safety goggles when doing this.)

2 Run hot water over the scored part of the bottle, followed immediately by cold water.

3 Pour more hot water over the glass and the end of the bottle should break off. Use sandpaper to smooth the cut. You could use the bottom part as a little bowl for trinkets.

4 Remove your chosen plant from its container and neatly secure the root-ball with moss and pieces of wire in order to create a compact ball that will fit inside the bottom of the bottle. Attach two pieces of wire to the root-ball, ensuring that they are long enough for you to thread them through the bottle ready for hanging.

5 Carefully thread the two long wires through the bottle, taking care not to damage the leaves of the plant.

6 Repeat the process for each bottle and then suspend the bottles from the ceiling. Hanging the bottles at different levels makes for a more eye-catching display.

HANGING FRUIT GARDEN

Hanging gardens are so on-trend at the moment. Not only do they make good use of available space, but they are also a stylish way to display your plants. They're also a wonderful means of creating your own small garden.

I used some sheet moss and garden twine to house the roots of the small, bright raspberry and kiwi bushes in the potting mix. You will need some sheet moss for each plant. Gently lay the moss on a flat surface and place a heap of potting mix on top so that it will sit underneath the plant's roots. Place the plant on top of the potting mix, envelop the roots with the moss, and secure it in place with garden twine. You will need to water your hanging garden regularly —I use the dip-and-drain method for about 10 minutes every day (see page 30).

as a child I remember summers spent picking fruit—it was one of my favorite treats. In this display, I wanted to re-create this sense of outdoor fun by hanging small raspberry and kiwi bushes outside the open kitchen doors

HANGING IVY

Bathrooms are ideal spots for indoor plants, as there can be ample space for an attractive display. Unfortunately, people often place dull artificial plants in a bathroom. However, if you think about it, the bathroom can be the most suitable room in the home for growing an indoor plant. In fact, the warm—often humid—conditions in a bright, well-lit bathroom are perfect for growing plants, even tropical ones.

Here, the lovely copper hanging container, which contains *Hedera helix* (ivy) underplanted with moss, creates a striking focal point in a relaxing bathroom. The ivy leaves peeking over the edge of the container are glossy and green and white, and look particularly bright against the neutral hues of the bathroom. If you are keeping plants in your bathroom, it's important to avoid spraying them with aerosols or dusting them with talcum powder or other bathroom products, as this can stop photosynthesis.

the **metallic beauty** of this bathroom container allows the variegated *ivy* to be shown in all its glory

long, delicate *tendrils* of *trailing ivy* form a waterfall of splendor beneath a lush **green** fern

IVY AND FERN HANGING BASKET

Hanging arrangements are a wonderfully creative way to display indoor plants. They create a fabulous point of interest in a living room, above a long table in a kitchen, or displayed in a hallway. This arrangement features lush, green, trailing *Hedera* (ivy) and busy *Nephrolepis exaltata* (Boston fern), both typically outdoor plants.

Hanging baskets are sweet reminders of country cottages, white picket fences, and roses around the front door. Here, however, this bountiful hanging basket makes a wonderful contrast to the crisp white surroundings of the room. Firstly, I took a hanging basket and removed the chain. I bought a longer chain from my local hardware store in order to create a much more dramatic hanging effect. I then took the coir lining from the hanging basket and sprayed it black to match the ironwork. I usually water my hanging basket outside, giving it a good soaking and then allowing the excess water to drain away, to avoid damaging the floor inside.

MACRAMÉ HANGING POTS

In the western hemisphere, macramé is thought to have originated among 13th-century weavers. These artisans knotted their excess thread and yarn to create decorative fringes on shawls, veils, and towels. Sailors then took up the craft while making objects at sea, and macramé spread to the New World. Although interest in macramé faded in after its revival in the 1970s, the craft is now enjoying a new burst of popularity.

The combination of terracotta pots and colorful macramé pot-holders is a stylish nod toward this regenerated trend. Here, I used three simple terracotta pots from a local garden center and three brightly colored macramé pot-holders from a small craft fair (have a look online for easy tutorials if you want to make one yourself). I planted the terracotta pots with exotic-looking *Guzmania*, a type of bromeliad. If possible, use only rainwater or distilled water for these plants, rather than tap water, and water the central cup instead of the potting mix. The arrangement looks fantastic hanging from the four-poster bed, which frames their intricate forms perfectly. What a beautiful sight to wake up to every day.

FRAMED MOSS

This is one of those displays that is guaranteed to wow visitors to your home; it's a really simple idea, but so striking! Here, I took three box picture frames and placed bun moss inside them. You need to keep the moss plants moist, so remember to spray them every day (for more information on growing moss, see page 99).

I also picked up this wonderful gilt frame from a flea market. It was while thinking up this display that it jumped into my mind, so I retrieved it from under the bed. I love the juxtaposition of the simple, modern, white frames with the ornate detail of the gold frame.

You will need to build a box behind the gilt frame to hold the *Sempervivum* succulents. To do this, I used some pieces of wood, which I cut to size. I then placed a piece of chicken wire over the top between the back of the picture frame and the top of the box and fixed it in place with a hot glue gun. The chicken wire holds the succulents firmly in position. Fill the box with potting mix to a depth of approximately 1in (3cm). You then simply poke the succulents through the holes in the wire and fill all the space in the picture frame with them.

allow a living wall of art to take center stage in a daring display, which exhibits a wealth of different textures

MOSS MASTERPIECE

This is a really fun display to create, and one that you can get the kids involved in as well. I think there is a lot to be said for turning your garden into a sort of outdoor room that you can decorate in much the same way as you would a room indoors. It becomes a place where you can sit, look about you, and relax.

This is a simple project to set up and uses a rectangular piece of hardboard. I painted the hardboard white, but you can use any color you wish and perhaps take inspiration from the surrounding garden plants.

Take some reindeer moss—I have used three different shades of green here. You could even spray-paint some of the pieces of moss with different colors to create a more interesting scene. Use a hot glue gun to fix the moss to the hardboard. There is no right or wrong way to position the moss; in fact, using different colors will mean you can be quite messy in your approach. This moss picture adds a lush feeling to the plain brick wall and brightens up a dark winter day!

with its striking combination of colors and textures, this painting of moss creates a stunning focal point on a garden wall

chapter 4

just outside

House plants are a wonderful way to bring some much-needed greenery into your home, but what about displays just outside? My favorite use for the garden is to turn it into an outdoor room. So, in this chapter, I have looked at decorating and adorning those little areas just outside a house or apartment, from windowsills to front doors, balconies to walled gardens. I really think you can have a lot of fun embellishing the spots immediately around your home.

symbolic foliage

Foliage provides some of the lushest decoration in the natural landscape. Often in the form of garlands, foliage has been used throughout history as a mark of celebration at weddings, christenings, traditional gatherings, and native celebrations, and also as religious offerings. It can be used to symbolize love, affection, peace, and respect.

Leaves have deep-rooted, symbolic meanings in many cultures. In China, for example, *Dracaena sanderiana* (lucky bamboo) is a symbol of prosperity. It is often used in feng shui—the Chinese practice of arranging buildings in relation to the flow of energy, as well as viewing the world as an interaction of five elements: water, fire, earth, wood, and metal. With its green color and thin vertical habit, lucky bamboo has all the characteristics of the element wood. Wood means growth and can be used to "grow" wealth, luck, or any other kind of positive outcome. So, lucky

ABOVE In China, *Dracaena sanderiana* (lucky bamboo) is a symbol of prosperity

LEFT AND OPPOSITE, TOP Ferns symbolize sincerity

bamboo is believed to attract a flow of positive energy wherever it is placed.

Hedera (ivy) leaves symbolize strong and lasting friendship because of their ability to remain attached to a surface in even the most inhospitable conditions. Other plants with symbolic foliage include *Aloe*, which represents healing, protection, and affection, and *Ocimum basilicum* (basil), a symbol of good wishes. In addition, ferns can mean sincerity; *Rosmarinus* (rosemary) stands for remembrance; *Chamaemelum nobile* (chamomile) means patience; and *Thymus* (thyme) is a symbol of courage and strength.

An excellent example of foliage at its best is the fall display in New England when maple trees, for example, put on a show of intense color, with red, gold, yellow, or orange leaves. This flaming beauty can be recreated at home by planting a maple in a large container and keeping it just outside.

RIGHT In the fall (autumn), the leaves of this *Acer palmatum* "Ukon" (a type of Japanese maple) will be a riot of fiery colors

the **composition** of these plants works so well and, as the plants grow, they will cover the **planting pockets** to create a lush living wall

LIVING WALL GARDEN

A living or "green" wall is defined as one that is partially or completely covered with vegetation and which includes a growing medium such as garden soil. Most "green" walls also feature an integrated water-delivery system. For this reason, they can be very difficult to maintain and keep properly watered, as well as extremely costly.

However, you do not have to invest in this way in order to create a stunning planted wall display. I have devised a great alternative here using these wall pockets that are readily available from garden stores to hold the plants. You really can create a fantastic scene with these vividly colored foliage plants.

Here, I chose some beautiful heucheras called "Midnight Rose," which provide a striking contrast to the lush greens of the *Adiantum* (maidenhair fern; pictured right) and *Dryopteris filix-mas* "l inearis Polydactyla," a type of hardy fern. The composition of these plants works so well and, as the plants grow, they will cover the planting pockets to create a lush living wall.

SHOCKING PINK AND GRAY

Gray and pink are always a great color combination—pink is such a fun, luscious shade and gray is a classy color, so together they can work wonders. I selected these beautifully bright azaleas and knew instantly that they would be the perfect match for the round zinc pot. Use an ericaceous potting mix, because azaleas don't like growing in soils that contain lime. This means that they won't grow well in soils with a high pH, which are referred to as alkaline.

TREE FERN CONTAINER

I found this speckled container at a lovely independent interiors and homeware store in the Cotswolds, England. It had a very different look from the other pots and containers in my collection. I tend to opt for zincs and other metals, so to choose another color and finish was quite a departure and leap of faith for me. I chose to plant a lovely tree fern, *Dicksonia antarctica*, in the pot and it looked at home immediately.

WINDOW **BOXES**

A blooming and bountiful window box will always brighten up an empty windowsill. Window boxes can be used to create an inviting approach to your property, and they help to turn a house into a home. They can be either characterful and busy or simple and streamlined, but all add a personal touch to your home's exterior.

When choosing a window box, I think it's important to bear in mind the external paintwork and windows of the property—do you want the box to blend in or clash with the decorative scheme? The light gray paint used here is striking and a very evocative color. Taking this into account, I decided to plant some lovely, pale pink *Hydrangea macrophylla* "Madame Emile Mouillère" to provide a gentle contrast with the colors of the house. The silver window box draws the whole look together.

SMALL-SPACE GARDENER

A small balcony or patio attached to a city apartment provides a little haven in an urban jungle. Decorated with pots and planters, flora and fauna, a city balcony can be a welcome green retreat. It's a good idea to put some garden furniture on your balcony—simply treat the space like a small outside room for entertaining and relaxing. I placed this lovely pot, which is planted with a large-flowered white hydrangea, on the table outside. It's a real attention-grabber among the vibrant green foliage.

frothing over the edge of an old **milk urn,** this selection of salad leaves will provide a bountiful summer feast

VEGETABLE GARDEN

While not strictly an indoor arrangement, this milk urn is the perfect example of a wonderful vintage find and upcycling. Lush, bountiful green lettuce always reminds me of Beatrix Potter's Peter Rabbit hiding from Mr. McGregor in a pretty market garden. I bought this milk urn from a fantastic antiques seller at a vintage market in Surrey, England. I wasn't sure what it could be used for or, more importantly at the time, how exactly I was going to get it home. Homegrown lettuces always taste better than store-bought specimens and, of course, are a lot more economical. I also planted scallions (spring onions) and beets (beetroot) in the urn. This large milk urn makes the perfect container for creating a tiny cottage garden of your own—just remember to check twice for a hiding Peter Rabbit!

PROVENÇAL CENTERPIECE

This dreamy arrangement of wistful wildflowers is a nod to long, hot summers spent in Provence, France. I arranged these beautiful sprays of pastel color in carefully selected vintage bottles and an aged wooden milk crate. The whole look has a charming, rustic appeal and is romantically reminiscent of a meadow walk or an afternoon exploring the French countryside. This is a lovely arrangement for an open kitchen or porch, but it would also make an unusual table arrangement for a picturesque, homespun wedding or perhaps a summer lunch just outside. (For further advice on cutting fresh flowers, see page 79.)

WAVING GRASSES

One day in the fall (autumn), while walking around a garden center, I was stunned to see these beautiful berries in an exquisite shade of purple. They belonged to a very hardy deciduous shrub called *Callicarpa bodinieri* var. *giraldii* "Profusion" (beauty berry), which flowers in summer, but then has these wonderful mauve berries in winter. I had never seen this color in nature before, so it was a must for me to buy it. Since it is such an architectural plant, I decided to pair it with something softer. For this reason, I chose two lovely *Pennisetum alopecuroides* "Hameln" (Chinese fountain grass), which is arguably one of the most elegant forms of this species of grass.

I completed the planting by top-dressing the potting mix with some moss. The red tones of the grasses really complement the subtle tone of the concrete container. This is a truly lovely composition, which works well either just outside the house or sitting on a garden wall.

DRYING FLOWERS

Air-drying is a great technique for drying most flowers, grasses, and seed heads. Remove all the leaves from each stem up to the flower head. I usually work on a bunch of flowers at a time.

Tie the flowers together with a rubber band so that the bunch will stay together when the stems contract. Only put a small number in a bunch, say 8 to 10 stems, so that they all dry equally and those in the middle don't rot. Hang the bunch upside down in a warm, dry, well-ventilated place such as an airing cupboard or basement. Leave the flowers until they are crisp.

In the example shown here, I have chosen to dry two roses. The rose is a prolific flower: the inspiration for countless literary quotations, a dramatic symbol of the Wars of the Roses (1455–87) in England, and the go-to flower for forgetful boyfriends on Valentine's Day. Roses are often written off for use in home interiors and floral arrangements because they appear so frequently and are universally popular. However, there are over a hundred very different varieties to choose from. The delicate petals of a rose can be very intricate and differ markedly from one variety to the next.

Drying roses is the perfect way to retain their romanticism and give them a wonderfully antiquated, vintage feel. I framed these two ivory rosebuds; their delicate mauve and pink lines make lovely points of interest. The black backdrop is a great contrast to the pretty buds.

To make these dried-flower pictures, you will also need to press the flowers for a couple of weeks. I only wanted to press them lightly, and so did not screw the press too tightly, in order to keep some of the form of the flowers. Or, more indecently, you can flatten them between the covers of a book under a table leg.

drying roses is the perfect way to retain their romanticism

PRESSING FLOWERS

Most leaves and flowers can be dried by pressing. Here, I used an old vintage press that I managed to obtain from a bric à brac store. Place the leaves and flowers in the press and cover with some blotting paper or newspaper. Smaller leaves can be placed on absorbent paper, such as kitchen paper, to speed up the drying process. Secure the press with the screws and leave for three weeks.

RESOURCES

United Kingdom

THE BALCONY GARDENER
020 7431 5553
www.thebalconygardener.com
One-stop shop for all your
small garden needs, including
container gardens, tools, outdoor
accessories, seeds, terrariums,
and vintage finds

ANTHROPOLOGIE
00800 0026 8476
www.anthropologie.eu
Garden accessories and
homeware

ETSY
www.etsy.com
Quirky container finds to house
your plants, plus terrarium kits

IKEA
08453 583363
www.ikea.com
Accessories, terracotta pots,
and glassware

United States and Canada

ANTHROPOLOGIE
Stores across the United States
(800) 309 2500
www.anthropologie.com
Garden accessories and
homeware

BEN WOLFF POTTERY
Connecticut
(860) 618 2317
www.benwolffpottery.com
Traditional and modern pottery

GRDN
Brooklyn, New York
(718) 797 3628
www.grdnbklyn.com
A complete store for the
urban gardener

JAYSON
Chicago, Illinois
(800) 472 1885
www.jaysonhome.com
Reclaimed pots and planters,
plants, and container planting

POTTERY BARN
Stores across the United States
(888) 779 5176
www.potterybarn.com
Outdoor lighting, garden
furniture, and outdoor tableware

ROLLING GREENS
Culver City and Los Angeles,
California
(310) 559 8656 or (323) 934 4500
www.rollinggreensnursery.com
Plants and containers

SPROUT HOME
Brooklyn, New York, and Chicago,
Illinois
(718) 388 4440 or (312) 226 5950
www.sprouthome.com
Contemporary garden center

TERRAIN AT STYERS
Glen Mill, Pennsylvania, and
Westport, Connecticut
(877) 583 7724
www.shopterrain.com
Assortment of stylish garden
supplies

WEST ELM
Stores across the United States
(888) 922 4119
www.westelm.com
Containers and terrariums

ACKNOWLEDGMENTS

First of all a huge, heartfelt thank you to Cindy, Sally, Gillian, and all the team at CICO for your belief in me, together with your guidance and patience in helping me create a book that I'm truly proud of. Thank you Helen, for your amazing photography and Marisa for your beautiful styling, the results of your hard work are plain for all to see. Endless thanks to my Mother, Father, Brother, and Grandfather, your continued love, support, and patience was integral to making this book possible, and to my Great Uncle Michael and his late wife Thelma's collection of house plant books which proved to be not only an inspiration but a great help too.

INDEX